BREEDING OURSELVES TO DEATH

LAWRENCE LADER

"THEIR BREEDING RATE IS INCREDIBLE."

Foreword by Dr. PAUL R. EHRLICH

"I highly recommend this book . . . Human population is the cause of most, if not all, of our ills."
—Arthur Godfrey

"The men and women now engaged in the struggle to control population will find the pioneering efforts described herein of great value to guide their work."
—General William H. Draper, Jr.

"This book is a significant contribution toward the educational process involved in bringing our population crisis to the attention of the American public."
—Senator Robert W. Packwood

BREEDING OURSELVES TO DEATH

30th ANNIVERSARY EDITION

LAWRENCE LADER

Foreword by Dr. Paul R. Ehrlich

SEVEN LOCKS PRESS

Santa Ana, California
Minneapolis, Minnesota
Washington, D.C.

For additional copies of this book please contact:

Negative Population Growth

1717 Massachusetts Ave. NW

Suite 101

Washington, DC 20036

(202) 667-8950

(202) 667-8953 Fax

www.npg.org   E-mail: npg@npg.org

Paperbound ISBN 1-931643-14-8

First Printing: March, 1971
Special Edition Printing 2002

Original cover art on page ii by Bill Mauldin: Copyright © 1967 by *Chicago Sun-Times*, reproduced courtesy of Wil-Jo Associates, Inc. and Bill Mauldin.
Special Edition Cover design by Sparrow Advertising & Design

Printed in the United States of America

Seven Locks Press
P.O. Box 25689
Santa Ana, CA 92799
(800) 354-5348

CONTENTS

October 23, 1969

Dear Mr. Moore:

The recent series of advertisements placed in
American newspapers by the Hugh Moore Fund
has been gratifying indeed. Your dedication to
easing the problems of world population growth
has led to a significant public service and the
people of the world are in your debt.

I especially appreciate your most recent effort.
Please convey my thanks and my personal regards
to the distinguished citizens who signed the statement, and accept my warmest wishes as you
continue your activities.

Sincerely,

Richard Nixon

Mr. Hugh Moore
The Hugh Moore Fund
60 East 42nd Street
New York, New York 10017

PREFACE

We are pleased to commemorate the 30th anniversary of NPG's founding by presenting this unique reprint of Lawrence Lader's *Breeding Ourselves to Death,* originally published in 1971.

To read Lawrence Lader's work 30 years after its first appearance is to be transported to a different time, a different mood, and a different national outlook. The book's initial publication coincided with the profoundly important recommendations of the Rockefeller Commission on Population Growth and the American Future. Presidents Kennedy, Johnson, and Nixon all had warned of the impact of global overpopulation, and the entire nation was energized and motivated on this clear and present danger. Indeed, there was a consensus on the problem at that time.

For those who may recall this book and Paul Ehrlich's *The Population Bomb,* glancing through these pages is an excursion back to an amazing time when concern over the world population explosion was dominant at all levels of government and media, as well as in the board rooms of the nation's corporations. Great figures like Dr. Paul Ehrlich, Hugh Moore, Dr. William Vogt, Rockefeller Prentice, Dorothy Brush, General William H. Draper, Jr., Ambassador Adolph W. Schmidt, Robert S. McNamara, and Senator Daniel Patrick Moynihan were visible, effective leaders for the vitally important cause we still fight for today. It was also a time when visionary leaders, like Don Mann—founder of Negative Population Growth—were moved to try to do more, to do as much as they could, indeed anything they could, to try to contain the world population growth rate. It was in this environment that NPG was founded. And it has been our good fortune to have Don Mann's leadership for these past 30 years.

For younger population activists, Lader's fascinating description of the work of the Hugh Moore Fund and its techniques is both a jolt and an inspiration. First the jolt: While the threat of overpopulation here and around the world is more urgent than ever, there is a stunning silence from United States domestic officials about this challenge. But now the inspiration: The work of the Hugh Moore Fund was dynamic and inspired. With vision and leadership, a small number of dedicated activists and visionaries were able to move overpopulation problems to the top of the United States domestic agenda. Using creative ad techniques, tireless lobbying and recruitment, and relentless drive to develop leadership at the highest levels of government, the movement chronicled here shows what kind of action can and must be sustained if we are ever to regain national prominence for the problems of United States and world overpopulation. It is an encouragement to us all.

We're honored to have Dr. Paul Ehrlich provide a new foreword to this edition, and we are deeply indebted to Sally Epstein and Don Collins for suggesting republication of this book at this time.

Sharon McCloe Stein
NPG executive director

FOREWORD

The term "population control" was still generally taboo in the American press at the midpoint of the Twentieth Century. Demographers discussed the spectacular rise of population in their cloistered halls. But the public at large was blissfully unaware that mankind faced a problem.

In the early nineteen fifties the Hugh Moore Fund, a non-profit educational foundation, distributed a pamphlet to the press and some 50,000 American leaders in the Who's Who calling attention to the flood of people engulfing the earth. The pamphlet, of which now more than a million and a half copies are in print, had—and is still having—an impact.

This book sets forth what happened. It is published as a historical record and with the hope that methods and techniques employed by the Hugh Moore Fund may be of use to the growing army of devoted men and women—and organizations—now engaged in the struggle to control the greatest menace of our time.

We must check the present unbridled population growth in order to stop the deterioration of our environment.

Paul R. Ehrlich
November, 1970

ADDENDUM 2001

In the more than three decades since I wrote the above, the world and its approach to the population problem have changed a great deal. On the positive side, birth rates have dropped dramatically in both rich and most poor nations. The drop among the rich has been especially welcome, since it has lessened their already disastrous impact on Earth's life support systems. On the negative side, world population has soared through six billion, and the United States has clearly claimed the title of "most overpopulated nation." With more than 285 million people and growing fast, it is now in third place in brute numbers, and with its high level of per capita consumption it is responsible for by far the greatest national share of global environmental destruction. And the sad thing is that population limitation (to say nothing of consumption control) has fallen off the government and public radar scopes in the United States. I hope that this book will help to elevate it again.

Paul R. Ehrlich
November, 2001

BREEDING OURSELVES TO DEATH

The Hugh Moore Fund, organized in 1944 to promote world peace, entered the population field early in the nineteen fifties with a pamphlet whose title provoked instant controversy.

The Population Bomb was the pamphlet's title and it used the phrase "population explosion" to describe the increasing numbers of people on earth.

That title and the closely associated phrase—both then entirely novel—are today on millions of lips and have become parts of the language, expressing the now widely accepted idea that over-population is the root cause of many environmental and social ills.

"Today the population bomb threatens to create an explosion as disruptive and dangerous as the explosion of the atom, and with as much influence on prospects for progress or disaster, war or peace," the pamphlet declared.

The booklet's whiplash phraseology stung a dormant public, and its relentless parade of facts and figures—about booming birth rates, looming famines, zooming taxes, all likely to breed war—made uncomfortable but compelling reading.

The increase in the population of the world has risen from 35 million to 70 million annually since the publication of the pamphlet. It is now recognized that we must reduce birth rates or await the inevitable disaster. We are on the way to *breeding ourselves to death*.

While many population experts fifteen years ago grasped the danger, they confined their warnings to erudite graphs for scholarly

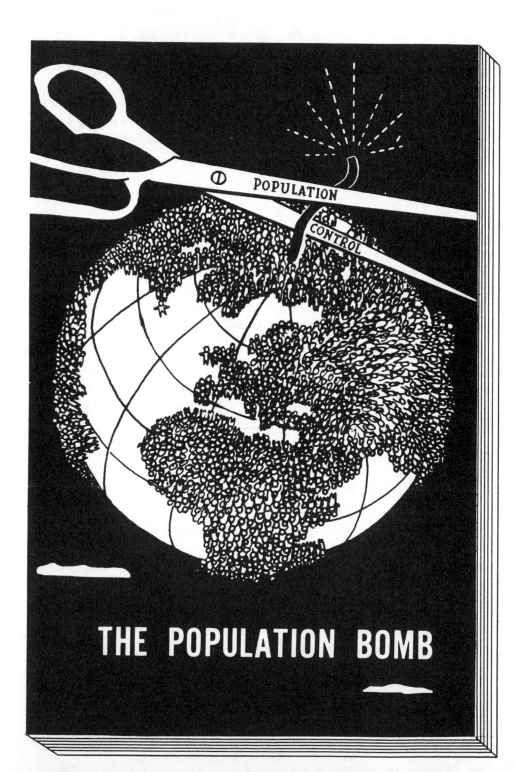

DR. ARNAUD C. MARTS, formerly President of Bucknell University and the dean of the fund-raising profession in the United States. As a director of the Hugh Moore Fund he was a sound adviser throughout the years of the Fund's activities in the population field.

Fabian Bachrach

circles. No one mentioned the impending disaster above a whisper. "Moore was way ahead of the experts," Dr. Arnaud Marts, former president of Bucknell University, commented.

The experts, in fact, considered publication of the pamphlet a mistake. John D. Rockefeller 3rd, chairman of The Population Council, felt that phrases like "population explosion" and "population bomb" might create an atmosphere of panic. Frederick Osborn, head of the Army's information and education program in World War II, urged that distribution of the pamphlet be halted.

Convinced, however, that India and many nations soon faced a frightening struggle between starvation and overpopulation, Hugh Moore thought the crisis too ominous to bury in academic treatises. A warning should be shouted from the rooftops.

His methods were often designed purposefully to stimulate controversy and thereby focus public attention. With time running out, people had to face raw facts. "Who among us," he liked to ask at meetings, "will come up with a plan for starting a CONFLAGRATION?"

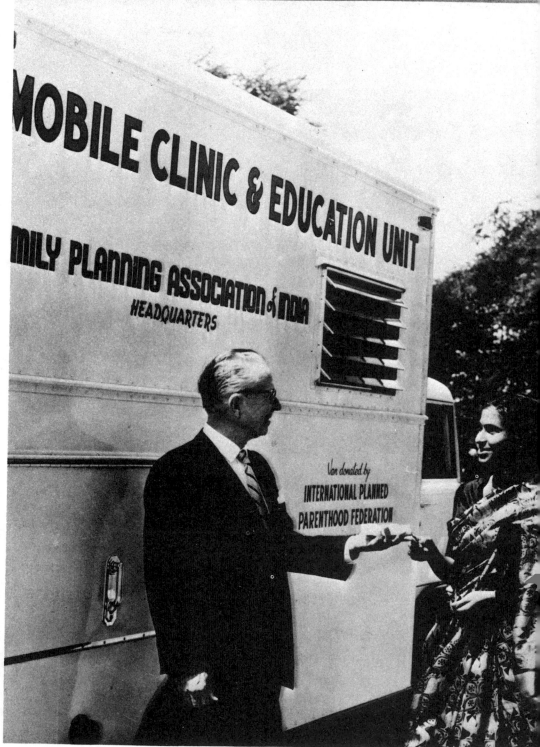

HUGH MOORE presents a mobile clinic to
the Family Planning Association of India.

DR. PAUL R. EHRLICH, Professor of Biology at Stanford University and popular spokesman for population control, is the author of the best-selling book on the subject, *The Population Bomb* (Sierra Club—Ballantine, over a million copies since 1968 publication). Ehrlich borrowed its title, with permission, from the 1954 Hugh Moore Fund pamphlet.

When the first printing of *The Population Bomb* reached a test-sampling of 1,000 leaders in business and the professions, reactions were surprisingly favorable. "The best presentation that I have seen of the basic threat to our civilization," Arthur Krock, dean of *The New York Times'* columnists, called it. "Although the contents of this booklet are frightening," wrote Roger H. Ferger, publisher of the *Cincinnati Enquirer,* "it should be read by every thinking American."

A 20,000 printing was followed by a third of 50,000. By 1967, the pamphlet had run through 13 editions. College professors had requested blocks of hundreds to use in their classrooms; ministers had praised it from their pulpits. The Nashville Tennessee *Banner* had reprinted it word for word on the editorial page of six consecutive issues. All told, by 1969, over 1,500,000 copies had been distributed in pamphlet form to leaders throughout the country.

"*The Population Bomb* riveted the attention of this generation on the problem," according to Harold Oram, a New York public

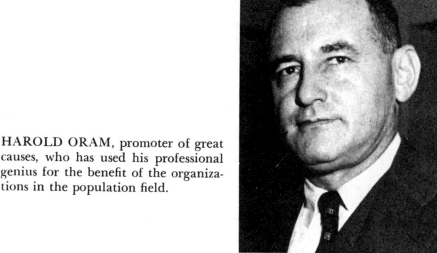

HAROLD ORAM, promoter of great causes, who has used his professional genius for the benefit of the organizations in the population field.

Fred Stein

relations expert in the health and welfare field. "It carried the greatest impact of any piece of population literature, and could well be called the *Uncle Tom's Cabin* of the movement."

In 1964, a decade after publication, Frederick Osborn agreed that the *Bomb* had helped change the climate of public opinion, enabling great foundations like Ford and Rockefeller together to concentrate over $100,000,000 on the population problem. "Moore was the first businessman willing to stand up and be counted on this issue, the first to stick his neck out," commented Dr. William Vogt, former national director of the Planned Parenthood Federation of America and author of the influential book, *The Road to Survival*, which first stirred Moore's interest in population.

Showman-Salesman for Population Control

If Hugh Moore deliberately used showmanship to hammer home his foundation's message, his principal techniques always remained

DR. WILLIAM VOGT, whose historic book *The Road to Survival* inspired the interest of the Hugh Moore Fund in the population problem.

Fabian Bachrach

those of the hard-headed businessman who had made a fortune analyzing and selling his market. As a young man he had founded an industry and made a product familiar to every American. Now he poured four decades of management and merchandising skills into the population movement with the same determination he had employed when, a few months out of Harvard, he peddled a bizarre idea—the paper cup. "The first day I went out and tried to sell a paper cup," he once reminisced, "the fellow looked at me and said, 'What's this for?' When we sold the business to American Can Company in 1957, forty million people a day were using Dixie cups."

Hugh Moore was the perfect complement to Margaret Sanger, the inspired pioneer of birth control. Both believed in daring tactics. Both rebelled against the suburban, tea-party aristocracy that had turned some planned parenthood groups into high-society enclaves. But beyond this, he added the priceless ingredients of business management and fund-raising skills. Only the unfortunate deterioration of Mrs. Sanger's health limited their alliance.

HUGH MOORE introduces Margaret Sanger to an audience in 1961 at the Waldorf-Astoria Hotel. This was Mrs. Sanger's last public appearance. At right is Sir Julian Huxley, the well-known British biologist and advocate of birth control.

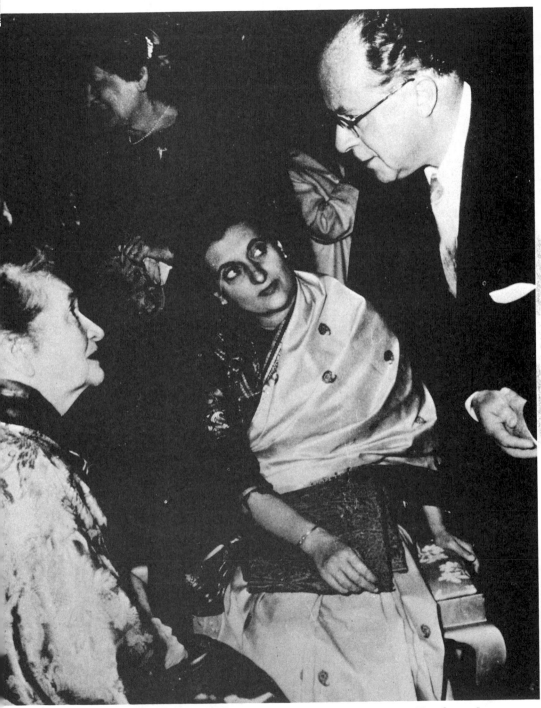

T. O. GRIESSEMER, Executive Director of the Hugh Moore Fund, confers with Margaret Sanger and Mrs. Indira Gandhi at the 6th International Conference on Family Planning of the International Planned Parenthood Federation at New Delhi in 1959.

In 1952, Mrs. Sanger succeeded in raising a small budget for the first world headquarters of the International Planned Parenthood Federation—a dingy suite on London's Eccleston Square with a staff of one and a part-time assistant. The world movement at this point actually consisted of a handful of devoted representatives from about a dozen countries, drawn together by Mrs. Sanger's magnetism. They generally met in her hotel room wherever she happened to be traveling. The Hugh Moore Fund's contribution was to lend the Federation executive strength.

In 1952 the Fund employed as director Tom O. Griessemer, a lawyer who had headed the world federalist movement's offices in New York and Geneva. The Fund paid Griessemer's salary but had him devote considerable time to the infant International Planned Parenthood Federation. At the 1953 Stockholm conference, Griessemer helped draw up IPPF's first constitution. Eventually he became secretary of IPPF's Western Hemisphere Region with offices in New York, and was one of the driving forces of the movement, attending every conference until his death in 1966.

Money and Men: Essential Partners

For Hugh Moore, the most glaring deficiency of the world population movement was its budget—a mere $35,000 annually as late as 1959. From the United States, the logical source of funds, the Planned Parenthood Federation of America, the American affiliate, contributed only $2,000 a year for work abroad.

Determined to put a solid financial base under IPPF, Moore launched the World Population Emergency Campaign with its first meeting at New Jersey's Princeton Inn on March 20, 1960. One observer has called this the "revolutionary turning-point" of the movement. It marked the emergence of three principal factors that increasingly characterized Moore's work.

Rejecting the hesitant, piecemeal approach of many planned parenthood groups, he stated the problem in huge historic terms.

JOSEPH SUNNEN, a Midwest tycoon who saw the need for birth control long before it became a popular cause. An inventor himself, he developed new devices and a new chemical to prevent conception. He spent hundreds of thousands of dollars on a pilot birth control project in Puerto Rico to learn if an operational formula could be found that might be applied in other, larger areas. He has also generously supported most of the organizations in the population field.

Barlow-Forrestal

The time had come to advance beyond the birth control clinic concept, mainly servicing the middle class. The scope was world-wide; the need of emergency proportions. From the dawn of history, the world only reached a population of two billions by 1930. It was expected to multiply to 14 billions by 2030. The rampant growth of population, in brief, now ranked with nuclear disaster as the greatest threat to peace on earth. "Hugh Moore brought a vivid sense of urgency to the movement," according to Elmo Roper, the noted public opinion authority.

The Hugh Moore Fund added a new kind of respectability by pulling into the Population Emergency Campaign a sizable contingent of financial and industrial leaders, such as Eugene Black of the World Bank; Will Clayton, cotton magnate and former Under Secretary of State; General William H. Draper, Jr., board chairman of Combustion Engineering and former Under Secretary of the Army; Marriner S. Eccles of the Federal Reserve Board; and Rockefeller Prentice. Moore not only wanted financial

ROCKEFELLER PRENTICE in-
herited his interest in the problems of
population from his father, Parmalee
Prentice, who wrote a book on hunger
long before it became a world problem. Rockefeller, like his cousin, John
D. Rockefeller 3rd, became one of the
leading supporters of population control as a means of checking the famine
that now stalks the earth.

Stuart-Rodgers Studios

support; he was following the tested merchandising principle that
controversial ideas need impeccable bedfellows.

A stellar recruit in the Fund's talent search was Lammot
duPont Copeland of the DuPont Company, later its chief executive. Moore discovered in his file a favorable letter from Copeland about *The Population Bomb* pamphlet. Then he arranged
for his banker, a fellow director of Copeland's on the Board of
the Pennsylvania Railroad, to introduce them. Copeland invited
Moore to lunch in Wilmington.

Described as "quite an occasion" by a mutual friend, the luncheon typified Moore's salesmanship. "He's a completely compelling
man," the friend commented. "His force is neither physical nor
vocal, but, in his quiet, determined way, he presents his ideas so
cogently and enthusiastically it becomes almost impossible to
disagree with him."

Not only did he persuade Copeland to join the committee con-
vening the Princeton meeting, but Copeland matched Moore's
initial donation of $10,000 "seed money" to launch the World

LAMMOT duPONT COPELAND, Chairman of E. I. duPont de Nemours & Co., Inc., the great chemical company, one of the important industrialists whom Hugh Moore interested in the population movement.

©Karsh, Ottawa

Population Emergency Campaign. Through the years since then, Copeland has emerged as one of the most beneficent supporters of the population movement, recently donating $2,000,000 to Harvard to inaugurate a Center for Population Studies.

The Princeton meeting raised $100,000 on the spot, and, in the next year or so, the Emergency Campaign enlisted a national membership of ten thousand. By the time it combined with the Planned Parenthood Federation in 1961 to form Planned Parenthood—World Population, the Emergency Campaign had turned over hundreds of thousands of dollars to Planned Parenthood for overseas work.

The culmination of this drive in May 1961 was a world tribute to Margaret Sanger at New York's Waldorf-Astoria hotel. Answering Moore's letter requesting her to make the long trip from Arizona to New York Mrs. Sanger replied: "You make me very, very happy. If humanly possible—if I have to crawl—I will be there."

She came and thrilled the large audience on the Starlight Roof with reminiscences of her early struggles in the days when she opened the first clinic in Brooklyn, and was jailed for doing it. That day in May 1961 saw the last public appearance of Margaret Sanger, one of the great women of her time.

As a member of the steering committee of the Emergency Campaign, Moore attracted such business luminaries to the population movement as Thomas S. Lamont of Morgan Guaranty Trust Company, and Fowler McCormick, chairman of International Harvester. The Waldorf meeting raised another $100,000 for birth control internationally. Today, in contrast to the gloomy balance sheet of 1959, the annual IPPF budget runs into millions of dollars.

After the Waldorf meeting, George Cadbury, a former United Nations official, wrote Moore it was "quite impossible to do justice to you and your hard work and the imagination you gave the whole event." And Mrs. Dorothy Brush, an early associate of Margaret Sanger and president of the Brush Foundation, concluded that he had "given International Planned Parenthood wings to get off the ground."

DOROTHY BRUSH, an early associate of Margaret Sanger. Mrs. Brush edited and published the International Planned Parenthood Federation *News,* which she mailed to I P P F affiliates throughout the world.

Population: A Government Responsibility

It became clear that the Fund's primary target should be to get the Federal Government committed to population control. The White House had long avoided the issue because of pressure from the Catholic hierarchy at home and sensitive relations with Catholic countries abroad.

A chance to break this taboo came when President Eisenhower in 1958 appointed a committee of ten prominent citizens to report on the effectiveness of U.S. foreign economic aid and its relationship to economic growth in every nation where we had mutual-assistance pacts. Among the committee members were John J. McCloy, former High Commissioner for Germany; General Alfred Gruenther, former Supreme Allied Commander in Europe, and General William H. Draper, Jr., the chairman.

Moore set out to convince Draper, an old friend, that economic aid was linked to population control. Millions of dollars in U.S. assistance were being wiped out when a beneficiary nation's population growth exceeded industrial and agricultural growth. In Latin America, he pointed out for example, despite increased food production in the previous five years, the average person was getting less to eat.

At a conference in his New York apartment, Moore heaped such statistics on Chairman Draper. The General's interest was undoubtedly caught, for he soon appointed Robert Cook of the Population Reference Bureau, of which Moore was chairman, as an official consultant to the Presidential committee. Cook and the Hugh Moore Fund proceeded to saturate committee members with material. "The climax was a seven-page telegram from Moore," Draper has recalled, "making it clear that if the committee didn't deal with the population issue we'd be derelict in our duty."

When the third section of the Draper report was published in 1959, population control received significant prominence. The decision had been made by a unanimous committee, including the Roman Catholic members.

DWIGHT D. EISENHOWER, who during his Presidency opposed government concern with population, later acknowledged the population explosion
as "one of the most critical world problems of our time," a danger to economic progress and to peace.

JAWAHARLAL NEHRU, Prime Minister of India, greeting Hugh Moore at the 1959 I P P F world conference in New Delhi. Between them are Mrs. Moore and Lady Rama Rau, President of the Family Planning Association of India.

ROBERT C. COOK, for many years the head of the Population Reference Bureau of which Hugh Moore was Chairman of the Board. His *Bulletins,* translating demographic facts into everyday language, were the most authoritative sources of information available and the basis for thousands of columns in newspapers throughout the world.

M. Graham Netting

It was a striking advance in public policy—the first official government report to take a stand on birth control. It brought the issue to national attention in the press, for *The New York Times* and many other papers focused on the population section of the report and featured a picture of Draper standing before a population chart. But he always credited Moore with this policy breakthrough, writing that Hugh Moore "practically forced the so-called Draper committee to speak its piece on population problems."

The Draper report also carried the issue to the public arena of religious debate. The Roman Catholic Bishops of the United States attacked it as part of a "systematic and concerted" campaign of "propaganda" for the use of foreign aid funds to encourage birth control in underdeveloped countries. On the other hand, a Protestant World Council of Churches' study group warned of the havoc of a "population explosion," urging birth control as one solution. The debate continued for months on the pages of the national press.

JOHN F. KENNEDY, who was the first American President to indicate concern with respect to the population problem.

In the end President Eisenhower rejected the population recommendations of the Draper report, insisting the government stay
out of family planning. It would be a few years before John F.
Kennedy, the first Catholic President, committed the government
to a hesitant population policy. By 1965, Eisenhower frankly reversed his position, advocating that the government join private
organizations in meeting "the great need of slowing down and
finally stabilizing the growth in the world's population." A year
later he applauded Congressional action giving "strong bipartisan
support for family planning programs here and overseas."

Advertising to the Many—and to One

With this opening wedge, the Hugh Moore Fund embarked in
1961 on a new strategy to push the government towards action in
the population field. The Fund began a series of full-page advertisements—the first ever devoted to the population problem. With
striking headlines, illustrations, and copy, they were designed to
reach government leaders through publication in *The New York
Times, The Washington Post, The Wall Street Journal* and *Time*
magazine. When it was learned on one occasion that President
Johnson would spend a long Christmas holiday at his Texas ranch,
the Fund made certain to catch the President's eye by running an
ad in the Austin (Texas) *American-Statesman* the Sunday after
Christmas.

Since the Fund linked population control to an immediate issue,
each ad had news-headline impact. When Congress debated the
foreign aid bill in 1963, the Fund appealed directly to President
Kennedy; "Population Explosion Nullifies Foreign Aid." The ad
aroused such comment that *The Reader's Digest* reprinted it as
an article, one of the rare times the *Digest* has run advertising text
as editorial copy.

The Fund moved almost as fast as the headlines. When President Johnson announced his "War on Poverty" in the State of the

10 E   THE NEW YORK TIMES, SUNDAY, JUNE 9, 1963.

POPULATION EXPLOSION NULLIFIES FOREIGN AID

An appeal to the President of the United States

We the undersigned citizens have supported the United States Foreign Aid program from the beginning for humanitarian and political reasons; but recent experience in many of the developing countries has shown that such aid is unavailing in the absence of some control of their exploding populations.

During the past five years the United States has paid out over 15 billion dollars in economic foreign aid to improve living standards in Asia, Africa and Latin America. Yet, by and large those standards have not risen and there are now over 250 million more people than there were five years ago —most of them hungry.

In the next five year period more than 15 billion dollars will doubtless be required in the effort to maintain the present dangerously low level of living of the enlarged populations. And in the period after that still more money will be needed unless the flood of new people is arrested. American economic aid, instead of ameliorating, may actually be compounding the economic problems of many of the overpopulated countries now receiving it.

ANOTHER ONE BILLION PEOPLE IN 15 YEARS

The population projection, as the chart shows, is appalling to contemplate. It took thousands of years from the time of the first man and woman to reach one billion people. That occurred about 1830. It required only one century to add the second billion—around 1930. It took less than **35 years** to add the third billion.

In the next 15 short years there will be still **another billion** people if the present rate of increase continues—most of them in countries now receiving U.S. aid.

This crop of newcomers would be greater than the total number of people living today in all the countries of Europe and North and South America. 1000 million more mouths to feed, bodies to clothe and house, minds to educate!

The resulting human misery and social tensions, we submit, would inevitably lead to chaos and strife—to many more Cubas and Haitis—to revolutions and wars, the dimensions of which it would be hard to predict. There would be no peace.

As for foreign aid in such a world, the question would appear to be at what point the U.S.—or for that matter the rest of the Great Powers of the West—will of necessity need to withdraw from a game of such rapidly mounting stakes.

WE RECOMMEND

With this prospect in mind it is our recommendation, Mr. President, that our own aid be continued for the time being on a carefully administered basis as proposed to you by the Clay Committee, but at the same time, **that the U.S. Government forthwith engage in a greatly accelerated program for limiting world population.**

We support the National Academy of Sciences in its request that the Government vastly expand research in the bio-medical aspects of human reproduction and the social aspects of population control. We agree with the Academy that "this problem can be successfully attacked by developing new methods of fertility regulation, and implementing programs of voluntary family planning widely and rapidly throughout the world," and that "the overall task is to achieve universal acceptance of the desirability of planning and controlling family size."

Mr. President, the position you took at your press conference last April 24 was encouraging. Also encouraging was the support our Government gave the Swedish Resolution on population control in the U.N. last December. You have correctly said that "the magnitude of the problem is staggering."

We therefore recommend specifically that you employ immediately the vast resources at your disposal through the National Institutes of Health and other Federal Agencies looking to a solution.

HUMANITY'S GREAT DILEMMA

We believe that the problem of rapid population growth ranks with that of thermonuclear arms as one of the two great dilemmas faced by modern man. At a time when this nation has programs involving the expenditure of $10 billion for the Alliance for Progress, $10 billion for space exploration and billions more for public health, it is tragic to contemplate the relatively infinitesimal sums now devoted to a problem upon the successful solution of which the others may well depend.

We heartily agree with you, Mr. President, that the U.S. should not impose birth control on other nations; but we would take a hard look at any applicant for economic aid who completely disregards the population factor.

POPULATION AID DESIRED

Many governments receiving U.S. economic aid today are thoroughly aroused to the problem of the mounting numbers of their people and would also happily accept aid from us in population control.

In conclusion, Mr. President, we make a judgment, to use your phrase, that the population problem dwarfs your current preoccupations with Laos, Berlin and the Atlantic Alliance—important as they are—and we believe that every day lost in tackling this matter on a massive scale will make its solution more difficult for you and your successors.

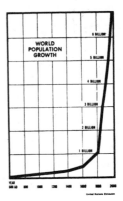

FRANK W. ABRAMS	New York, N.Y.	RAY P. DINSMORE	Akron, Ohio	THOMAS S. LAMONT	New York, N.Y.
WINTHROP W. ALDRICH	New York, N.Y.	WILLIAM H. DRAPER, JR.	Palo Alto, Calif.	CHAUNCEY D. LEAKE	Columbus, Ohio
JACQUES BARZUN	New York, N.Y.	ALEXANDER E. DUNCAN	Baltimore, Md.	HERBERT H. LEHMAN	New York, N.Y.
RUSSELL BENNETT	Minneapolis, Minn.	MARRINER S. ECCLES	Salt Lake City, Utah	CLARENCE COOK LITTLE	Trenton, Me.
WALTER J. BERGMAN	New York, N.Y.	HARRY EMERSON FOSDICK	Bronxville, N.Y.	JOHN L. LOEB	New York, N.Y.
EUGENE R. BLACK	New York, N.Y.	ARTHUR B. FOYE	New York, N.Y.	ARCHIBALD MacLEISH	Cambridge, Mass.
JACOB BLAUSTEIN	Baltimore, Md.	CHAUNCEY B. GARVER	Oyster Bay, N.Y.	ARNAUD MARTS	Whitehouse, N.J.
DONALDSON BROWN	Fort Deposit, Md.	MRS. WALTER S. GIFFORD	Greenwich, Conn.	MRS. CORDELIA SCAIFE MAY	Ligonier, Pa.
ARTHUR H. BUNKER	New York, N.Y.	A. CRAWFORD GREENE	San Francisco, Calif.	FOWLER McCORMICK	Chicago, Ill.
HENRY B. CABOT	Boston, Mass.	LELAND HAZARD	Pittsburgh, Pa.	ASHLEY MONTAGU	Princeton, N.J.
STUART CHASE	Georgetown, Conn.	FANNIE HURST	New York, N.Y.	CRAIG MOORE	Easton, Pa.
WILL L. CLAYTON	Houston, Texas	ANCEL KEYS	Minneapolis, Minn.	REINHOLD NIEBUHR	New York, N.Y.
RANDOLPH P. COMPTON	Scarsdale, N.Y.	SHERMAN R. KNAPP	Kensington, Conn.	FAIRFIELD OSBORN	New York, N.Y.
DONALD K. DAVID	Osterville, Mass.	JOSEPH WOOD KRUTCH	Tucson, Ariz.	GREGORY PINCUS	Shrewsbury, Mass.
AUGUST DERLETH	Sauk City, Wis.	RICHARD S. KYLE	Wayne, N.J.	ROCKEFELLER PRENTICE	Chicago, Ill.
	LAWRENCE WILKINSON	New York, N.Y.		DON YOST	

WHITELAW REID	Purchase, N.Y.
JOHN ROCK	Brookline, Mass.
ELMO ROPER	New York, N.Y.
ADOLPH W. SCHMIDT	Pittsburgh, Pa.
CHARLES E. SCRIPPS	Cincinnati, Ohio
GEORGE C. SHATTUCK	Boston, Mass.
HENRY KNOX SHERRILL	Boxford, Mass.
WILLIAM B. SHOCKLEY	Los Altos, Calif.
ERNEST L. STEBBINS	Baltimore, Md.
SIDNEY A. SWENSRUD	Ligonier, Pa.
CHARLES P. TAFT	Cincinnati, Ohio
WILLIAM H. VANDERBILT	Chestnut Hill, Mass.
MARK VAN DOREN	Falls Village, Conn.
HAMILTON M. WARREN	Washington, Conn.
PASCAL K. WHELPTON	Oxford, Ohio

For more detailed information about the population explosion titles of reference works and the addresses of organizations in the field, write
The Hugh Moore Fund, 51 East 42nd Street, New York 17, N.Y.

For signers' "who's who"
see back of sheet   THE NEW YORK TIMES

WAR ON POVERTY

To President Lyndon B. Johnson

We the undersigned citizens salute you, Mr. President, upon your declaration of "unconditional war here and now on poverty...not only to cure it but to **prevent it.**"

To win this war you will need to tackle a root cause of poverty—**the present explosive growth of population.** We will have another 150 million people in the United States in 36 short years at the current rate of increase.

This presents the prospect of 8 million unemployed instead of 5 million today—of 10 million on welfare, of 30 million elderly and 100 million children to be taken care of. The cost of maintaining such an enlarged burden of non-producers could of itself add millions of families to those which today are unable to adequately support themselves.

However, Mr. President, competent authorities assert that a crash program vigorously supported by the government could arrest the population explosion. If you could thereby uncover the answer to the American dilemma through research you may also be able to help scores of poverty-ridden nations dependent upon the U.S. for economic aid.

WORLD POPULATION SKYROCKETS

The worldwide population projection, as the chart shows, is appalling to contemplate. There would be one billion—**1000 million!**—more people on earth in the next 15 years.

This incredible increase of mankind would be greater in numbers than all the people **now** living in the 55 countries of Europe and the entire Western Hemisphere taken together.

SCIENTISTS SPEAK

The National Academy of Sciences, the nation's leading scientific body, has declared "that the population problem can be successfully attacked by developing new methods of fertility regulation and implementing programs of voluntary family planning widely and rapidly throughout the world."

Today the U.S. Government is spending less than $10 million on this basic problem out of an annual budget of $15 billion for research. This amount is less than 1% of the expenditure for the Alliance for Progress and less than 1% of the cost of putting a man on the moon by 1970!

NOT A POLITICAL MATTER

President Kennedy at a news conference shortly before his death said that "we should know more and do more about the whole reproductive cycle and this information should be available to the world."

President Eisenhower has recently commented that "the time has come when we must take into account the effect of the population explosion on our mutual assistance system. Unless we do, it may smother the economic progress of many nations."

Richard Nixon has declared that he had seen poverty in Asia "worse than I have ever dreamed existed" and recommended that the U.S. give assistance in population matters to nations requesting it.

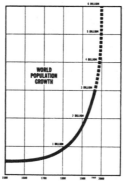

WORLD POPULATION GROWTH

NOT A RELIGIOUS MATTER

Pope Pius XII said "the regulation of offspring is compatible with the law of God" and called for extensive research to improve the rhythm method. Father John O'Brien, Professor of Theology at Notre Dame University, has declared that the **major faiths** joined in recognizing the need for a "prudent regulation of births...".

Senator Joseph Clark of Pennsylvania, after his re-election, said on the floor of the Senate "...there is a rather substantial Catholic population in my State. I received no adverse criticism of any consequence because I was advocating positive research and discussion in this area. Many of our colleagues who are inclined to hold back in that area need really feel no serious concern that what they will do will have an adverse effect on their political life."

One thing is certain, Mr. President, 35 million Americans — "one-fifth of all families with incomes too small to meet their basic needs" — will support you in your war on poverty.

WE RECOMMEND

1. That you promptly exercise the authority given you by the foreign aid bill which you signed January 7 "to conduct research into the problems of population growth."

2. That you wholeheartedly support the Concurrent Resolution of Messrs. Clark and Gruening in the Senate, to wit:

a. That the President speedily implement the policy of the U.S. regarding population growth as declared before the United Nations by inaugurating substantially increased **programs of research** within the National Institutes of Health.

b. That the President create a Presidential Commission on Population which shall be charged with the duty to inform, after investigation, the government and the American people of the nature of population problems with respect to the implications on all aspects of American life.

* * * * *

Mr. President, unless corrective measures are taken "here and now", the resulting human misery and social tensions will inevitably lead to chaos and strife at home and abroad—to more Panamas, Haitis and Cubas—to revolutions and wars, the dimensions of which it would be hard to predict. All of it grist for the Communist mill.

There would be no peace.

FRANK W. ABRAMS .... New York, N. Y.
GEORGE V. ALLEN .... Washington, D. C.
THURMAN W. ARNOLD .... Washington, D. C.
JACQUES BARZUN .... New York, N. Y.
WALTER J. BERGMAN .... New York, N. Y.
EUGENE R. BLACK .... New York, N. Y.
JACOB BLAUSTEIN .... Baltimore, Md.
THOMAS C. BOUSHALL .... Richmond, Va.
PERCIVAL F. BRUNDAGE .... Pompano Beach, Fla.
LAMAR BURDICK .... Wilmington, Del.
HENRY B. CABOT .... Boston, Mass.
STUART CHASE .... Georgetown, Conn.
WILL L. CLAYTON .... Houston, Texas
RANDOLPH P. COMPTON .... Scarsdale, N. Y.
JAMES A. CRABTREE .... Pittsburgh, Pa.
AUGUST DERLETH .... Sauk City, Wis.
RAY P. DINSMORE .... Akron, Ohio
BENEDICT J. DUFFY .... Washington, D. C
MARRINER S. ECCLES .... Salt Lake City, Utah

THEODORE EDISON .... West Orange, N. J.
JAMES M. FAULKNER .... Boulder, Colo.
HARRY EMERSON FOSDICK ...... Bronxville, N. Y.
ARTHUR B. FOYE .... New York, N. Y.
I. HENRY GARLAND .... San Francisco, Calif.
CHAUNCEY B. GARVER .... Oyster Bay, N. Y.
MRS. W. ST. JOHN GARWOOD ... Austin, Texas
A. CRAWFORD GREENE .... San Francisco, Calif.
LELAND HAZARD .... Pittsburgh, Pa.
F. PEAVEY HEFFELFINGER ..... Minneapolis, Minn.
FANNIE HURST .... New York, N. Y.
SHERMAN R. KNAPP .... Kensington, Conn.
JOSEPH WOOD KRUTCH .... Tucson, Ariz.
RICHARD S. KYLE .... Wayne, N. J.
THOMAS S. LAMONT .... New York, N. Y.
CHAUNCEY D. LEAKE .... Columbus, Ohio
MARX LEVA .... Washington, D. C.
ARTHUR C. LICHTENBERGER .... Greenwich, Conn.
DAVID E. LILIENTHAL .... New York, N. Y.

CLARENCE COOK LITTLE .... Trenton, Me.
JOHN L. LOEB .... New York, N. Y.
HENRY L. LOGAN .... Bronxville, N. Y.
MRS. CLARE BOOTHE LUCE ..... New York, N. Y.
ARNOLD H. MAREMONT .... Chicago, Ill.
ARNAUD C. MARTS .... Whitehouse, N. J.
MRS. CORDELIA SCAIFE MAY ... Ligonier, Pa.
FOWLER McCORMICK .... Chicago, Ill.
MRS. STANLEY McCORMICK ..... Boston, Mass.
CRAIG MOORE .... Easton, Pa.
LLOYD MORAIN .... San Francisco, Calif.
WILLIAM E. MORAN, JR. ...... Washington, D. C.
CLIFFORD C. NELSON .... New York, N. Y.
ALLAN NEVINS .... San Marino, Calif.
JOHN NUVEEN .... Chicago, Ill.
FAIRFIELD OSBORN .... New York, N. Y.
GREGORY PINCUS .... Shrewsbury, Mass.
MRS. FRANCIS T. P. PLIMPTON New York, N. Y.
ROCKEFELLER PRENTICE ...... Chicago, Ill.

WHITELAW REID .... Purchase, N. Y.
JOHN ROCK .... Brookline, Mass.
ELMO ROPER .... New York, N. Y.
ADOLPH W. SCHMIDT .... Pittsburgh, Pa.
CHARLES E. SCRIPPS .... Cincinnati, Ohio
GEORGE C. SHATTUCK .... Boston, Mass.
HENRY KNOX SHERRILL .... Boxford, Mass.
WILLIAM SHOCKLEY .... Los Altos, Calif.
ERNEST L. STEBBINS .... Baltimore, Md.
LEWIS L. STRAUSS .... Washington, D. C.
SIDNEY A. SWENSRUD .... Ligonier, Pa.
CHARLES P. TAFT .... Cincinnati, Ohio
HAROLD C. UREY .... La Jolla, Calif.
WILLIAM H. VANDERBILT ..... Chestnut Hill, Mass.
MARK VAN DOREN .... Falls Village, Conn.
PAUL K. WHELPTON .... Oxford, Ohio
LAWRENCE WILKINSON .... New York, N. Y.
JOHN R. WYON .... Boston, Mass.
DON M. YOST .... Pasadena, Calif.

To Readers: If you wish to register your support of the foregoing appeal write to: Hugh Moore Fund, 51 East 42nd Street, New York, N.Y. 10017

THE NEW YORK TIMES

THREAT
to
"THE GREAT SOCIETY"

To President Lyndon B. Johnson

In your Madison Square Garden speech you said that "this generation has man's first opportunity to create 'The Great Society.'" To achieve that goal, Mr. President, you will need to deal with an underlying cause of human misery and unrest—the rocketing growth of population.

The Population Bomb is fast becoming one of the major concerns of the American people—ranking with the atomic bomb. Newspapers and magazines devote columns every day to it, and for good reason. We will have 150 to 200 million more people in the United States in the next 35 years at the present rate of increase. This presents the prospect of 8 million unemployed—instead of 5 million today—of 10 million on welfare, 30 million elderly and 100 million children to provide for.

Reporting the increase of 63 million people in the world last year, the New York Times said editorially:

"This news is just as important as any this newspaper can print - it was indeed headlined on our front page. It means more in the long run than elections, economic trends, catastrophies and international crises. If the human race is to survive on anything higher than a slum basis, something will have to give—presumably the birth rate. Such is today's biggest news—and greatest problem."

The world population projection, as the cha . shows, is appalling to contemplate. At the present rate of increase, in another 15 short years there will be one billion—one thousand million!—more people on earth.

This incredible proliferation of mankind would be greater in numbers than all of the people now living in the 55 countries of Europe and the entire Western Hemisphere taken together!

The National Academy of Sciences, the nation's leading scientific body, has declared that "the population problem can be successfully attacked by developing new methods of fertility regulation and implementing programs of voluntary family planning widely and rapidly throughout the world."

President Kennedy, at a news conference shortly before his death, said, that "we should know more and do more about the whole reproductive cycle, and this information should be available to the world." Today the U.S. government is spending less than $10 million on this basic problem in an annual budget of $15 billion now spent for research—less than 1% of the expenditure for the Alliance for Progress and less than 1% of the cost for putting a man on the moon by 1970!

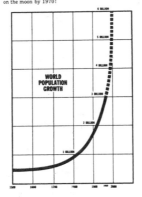

WORLD POPULATION GROWTH

WE RECOMMEND

Mr. President, the American people have overwhelmingly asserted their confidence in you—in your judgment and your proven courage to deal forthrightly with any problem affecting the country's wellbeing. We, the undersigned citizens, applaud your high resolve to create The Great Society and to that end respectfully recommend that you take the following steps:

1. That you place the Population Problem on the agenda of the White House Conference which you promised during the campaign to explore every means to preserve world peace.

2. That you include family planning in the Economic Opportunity program to alleviate U.S. poverty, for which you have at your disposal an appropriation of nearly one billion dollars.

3. That you direct our Mission at the United Nations to provide vigorous leadership looking to a solution of the world population problem, including technical aid.

4. That you inaugurate a substantial research program in the Department of Health, Education and Welfare in conformity with President Kennedy's proposal.

Mr. President, unless drastic measures are taken promptly, hunger, human misery and social tensions will undermine your Great Society. The population explosion will inevitably lead to chaos and strife at home and abroad —to more Cubas and Viet Nams—to revolutions and wars, the dimensions of which it would be hard to predict. All of it grist for the Communist mill.

There would be no peace!

Readers wishing to associate themselves with this statement may write the Hugh Moore Fund, 60 East 42nd St., New York, N. Y. 10017

THE NEW YORK TIMES

Famine stalks the earth

Too many people!

To President Lyndon B. Johnson

"The world is on the threshold of the biggest famine in history," according to Dr. Raymond Ewell, former advisor to the Government of India. "If present trends continue, it seems likely that famine will reach serious proportions in India, Pakistan and China in the early 1970s. Such a famine will fall in this category by 1980. Such a famine will be of massive proportions, affecting hundreds of millions, possibly billions of persons."

The Director-General of the United Nations Food and Agriculture Organization, Mr. Binay Sen, said recently: "Either we take the fullest measures both to raise productivity and to stabilize population growth, or we face a disaster of unprecedented magnitude. In some of the most heavily populated areas the outbreak of serious famines in the next five to ten years cannot be excluded. Problems of hunger and malnutrition which afflict more than a half of the world's population, apart from the human suffering and human degradation that they involve, pose a serious threat to peace."

U.S. Secretary of Agriculture, Mr. Orville L. Freeman, said: "Problems of staggering proportions face the densely populated underdeveloped countries of the world in their effort to keep food production in pace with population growth. Both land and time are running out for those countries. In the past, increases in food output were achieved by putting new land under cultivation. But now the supply of readily cultivatable land is nearly exhausted in many of those countries, and new land can be brought under cultivation only at high cost."

A generation ago Latin America, Asia and Africa were regions with food surpluses. They exported grain to the industrialized countries, especially to Europe. Now the food flow is reversed and they must import food.

Food into a bottomless pit

The United States has shipped abroad, since Congress enacted the so-called "Food For Peace" law in 1954, food products amounting to *the gigantic sum of $12 billion*, mostly on a give-away basis.

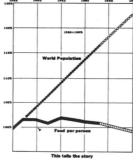

This tells the story

Our food warehouses that were bursting at the seams a few years ago are now largely down to a normal inventory required for reserves. Congress recently authorized Secretary Freeman to go into the open market and buy dried milk to keep up our lunch program for overseas children.

India receives from the United States more than a half of

its wheat at the present rate of 20,000 tons a day. Observers believe that this assistance is the only barrier against large scale famine and open rebellion.

With all this out-pouring of American resources we are not making a dent at solving the problem. Even if we were to continue such a program on a vastly stepped up basis, as some suggest, until American farm lands were exhausted, we still could not feed the burgeoning billions of people.

Basic problem: skyrocketing population

Everything possible, of course, should be done to increase the food supply, but *it is the skyrocketing population that menaces today's world*. Latin America, as an example, increased its total production of food over the last five years, but with 25 million more people, the *average individual had 7% less to eat*. And in another five years at the present rate of increase there will be 35 million *more people* living south of the Rio Grande.

Mr. President, we applaud your statement to the United Nations last June in which you said "Let us in all our lands—including this land—face forthrightly the multiplying problems of our multiplying populations and seek the answers to this *most profound challenge to the future of all the world*."

But the fact remains that to date the manpower and resources of the various agencies of the Government committed to meet this transcendent challenge rank below a hundred less important projects.

Every day lost in tackling this matter on a massive scale will compound your problems and those of your successors. For you were right, Mr. President, when you said:

"I do not believe that our island of abundance will be finally secure in a sea of despair and unrest, or in a world where even the oppressed may one day have access to the engines of modern destruction."

There will be 300 million more mouths to feed in the world five years from now—most of them hungry. Hunger brings turmoil and turmoil, as we have learned, creates the atmosphere in which the communists seek to conquer the earth.

Union message of January 8, 1964, it quickly addressed another open letter to the President in a full-page newspaper ad: "To win this war you will need to tackle a root cause of poverty—the present explosive growth of population."

After President Johnson's "Great Society" speech later that year, the Fund captioned its ad, "Threat to the Great Society," specifically recommending that family planning be included in the new Economic Opportunity program, and that the U.S. government take the lead in population control at the United Nations.

In 1965, as starvation in India became a frightening reality, Dr. Raymond Ewell, former advisor to the government of India predicted, "The world is on the threshold of the biggest famine in history." Dr. Binay Sen, Director-General of the U.N.'s Food and Agriculture Organization, warned of "a disaster of unprecedented magnitude."

Taking such authoritative conclusions as a theme, the Fund's next ad was headlined: "Famine Stalks the Earth." Despite a vast outpouring of American food to India and other nations, the ad argued, we could not make "a dent at solving the problem" without population control.

A significant aspect of each ad was that it represented not only the opinion of the Hugh Moore Fund, but of the score of American leaders who signed it. These names contributed substantial weight to every statement—business leaders such as Frank W. Abrams, former chairman Standard Oil Company of New Jersey and Henry Ittleson, Jr., chairman, C.I.T. Financial Corporation; government officials such as Ambassador Winthrop Aldrich and Admiral Arthur W. Radford, former chairman, Joint Chiefs of Staff; Nobel Prize winners Dr. Linus Pauling and Dr. William Shockley; authors Allan Nevins and Joseph Wood Krutch.

The Fund was determined to bring pressure on Washington not only through the ads, but through an outpouring of letters from all over the country. Every reader who returned a coupon supporting the ad's position received a personal letter from Hugh Moore, urging him to write policy makers in Washington. As a

LYNDON B. JOHNSON, who as President alerted the American public with his repeated statements regarding the danger of the population explosion.

result, Senators and Representatives—probably for the first time—got a barrage of mail from their constituents, urging action on the population problem.

The response from Congressmen to these constituents gave an accurate picture of Congressional opinion. In 1966, for example, 87 Senators and 228 Representatives in 45 states indicated strong or moderate support for stepped-up government programs on population.

The Fund in those days had no measure of its own impact in relation to the pressure for population control from other segments of society. Still, there were meaningful indexes. Senator Edward M. Kennedy of Massachusetts, for example, straddled the population issue in a dozen replies he sent to the constituents who first approached him. But by the end of the year he changed his mind, writing, "I share your concern and interest in bringing the world's population in balance with world resources, and shall support legislative action in this area."

Similarly, no political analyst could fathom the complex decision-making process in the Johnson White House or how the Fund's campaigns affected it.

Nevertheless, shortly after the "Great Society" ad, Special Assistant Bill D. Moyers stated, "The questions raised by the open letter to the President are currently receiving serious study by various interested agencies within the government." Coincidentally or not, President Johnson announced a few weeks later in his State of the Union message: "I will seek new ways to use our knowledge to help deal with the explosion in world population and the growing scarcity in world resources."

Again, not long after another Fund ad insisted that millions of dollars in foreign aid went down a "rathole" when population increased faster than food supply, the President declared: "Let us act on the fact that less than five dollars invested in population control is worth a hundred dollars invested in economic growth."

THE NEW YORK TIMES

Catholic Bishops assail birth control as millions face starvation

The charges of the Roman Catholic Bishops on November 14 add up to a frontal attack on organized family planning.

The Bishops called upon everyone: "to oppose, vigorously and by every democratic means, those campaigns already underway in some states and at the national level toward the active promotion, by tax-supported agencies, of birth prevention as a public policy, above all in connection with welfare benefit programs."

This aggressive move was made notwithstanding the known facts respecting the population explosion which President Johnson has called "humanity's greatest challenge."

Tidal wave of people

A tidal wave of *three billion* more people will inundate the earth in the next 30 years, *if the present rate of increase is not arrested!*

The population of the United States may increase by 150 million!

Famine already stalks the earth. India, kept from the brink today by U.S. wheat shipments, will add 200 million more people by 1980.

"The world is on the threshold of the biggest famine in history," concludes Dr. Raymond Ewell, former advisor to the Government of India. Dr. Ewell predicts famine in India, Pakistan and Communist China about 1970, and in Brazil, Egypt, Indonesia, and Turkey shortly after.

The Bishops' accusation goes beyond their unsupported charges of coercion of women on welfare. It encompasses all family planning, *domestic and international*. It strikes at "our Government's stepped-up intervention in family planning, including the subsidizing of contraceptive programs at home and abroad...."

World catastrophe in prospect

If the Bishops succeed in their attempt:
1. Millions of women on welfare would be deprived of the knowledge and effective methods of preventing the birth of children they cannot care for.
2. Through fear of reprisal at the polls, state legislators may hold back welfare funds for family planning, thereby increasing the tax burden of unwanted children.
3. Federal administrators, whose "stepped-up" programs the Bishops have attacked, may cut or diminish these programs.
4. The President of the United States himself is threatened by the Bishops' warning that *"our public officials be on guard..."*
5. Congressmen may hesitate to advance the program on for-

EMPTY BOWL

HUNGER

eign aid in the population field so splendidly begun by the 89th Congress. Without population control the huge *$7 billion* Food for Peace program will be a mere stop-gap, saving the lives of those who would produce still more hungry people.

"Either we take the fullest measures both to raise productivity and to stabilize population growth, or we face a disaster of unprecedented magnitude," according to Dr. B. R. Sen, Director-General of the United Nations Food and Agriculture Organization.

If such measures are not taken, it is likely that Americans — a humane people — may be rationing the food on their own tables in the not distant future.

Public favors birth control

John F. Kennedy was the first U.S. President to concern himself officially with the problem of population limitation.

The Bishops' attack has been read by enlightened Catholic leaders with a sense of unbelief and dismay. They have called it unrealistic, out-of-date, reactionary and inconsistent with the spirit of Vatican II in the modern world. Professor William D'Antonio of Notre Dame University referred to the Bishops' statement as "beating a dead horse."

Asked in a Gallup survey last year if birth control information ought to be easily available to any married person wanting it, *81 per cent of Catholics and 86 per cent of non-Catholics said YES.*

The battle will be won

The National Academy of Sciences, the nation's leading scientific body, has declared that "the population problem can be successfully attacked by developing new methods of fertility regulation and implementing programs of voluntary family planning widely and rapidly throughout the world."

The magnitude of the challenge, however, is so great that only Government can meet it fully. The National Council of Churches has come out against any government curtailment of "its efforts to provide increasingly adequate services for all families or governments where such services are desired."

Individuals and organizations should speak out quickly in vigorous support of the Government's present program. Contact Federal, State and City officials. Point out that the American people—Catholics, Protestants and Jews—are overwhelmingly behind the program, as every poll shows.

Birth control is a popular cause which can be supported confidently.

If in the years to come the earth should be ravished by the fabled horsemen of the Apocalypse—War, Famine, Disease and Death—let the responsibility not be ours.

HUGH MOORE FUND
60 East 42nd Street
New York, N.Y. 10017

1. I subscribe wholeheartedly to this statement.
2. Please send me _____ reprints without charge.
3. Add my name to your mailing list for further information.

NAME _____

ADDRESS _____

CITY _____ STATE _____ ZIPCODE _____

Those signing this statement do so in their personal and individual capacity. The institutional and business affiliations are purely descriptive carrying no implication of authorization or participation by the organization noted.

This message may be quoted in whole or in part with or without credit. Reprints and mats of the advertisement are available without charge.

Meeting the Church Head-On

As the President slowly felt his way towards further population programs, the Catholic hierarchy reacted violently and unexpectedly in November 1966. All Catholic Bishops in the United States joined together in an attack on government support of family planning. Its bitterness was reminiscent of an era decades earlier when Catholic churchmen pilloried Margaret Sanger.

The immediate point of the Bishops' attack was alleged pressure for the adoption of contraception by welfare agencies on their clients. No specific instances or pressure, however, were cited. Most liberal Catholics considered the polemic outdated and, in the words of Professor William D'Antonio of Notre Dame University, "beating a dead horse."

The Hugh Moore Fund concluded that the Bishops had gone far beyond the welfare issue. The statement encompassed all family planning, domestic and international, striking at "our government's stepped-up intervention in family planning, including the subsidizing of contraceptive programs at home and abroad. . . ."

Since the Bishops had urged that "our public officials be on guard," Moore saw real danger that Congressmen would hesitate to vote funds for family planning programs, and that local welfare funds for birth control could be stifled by Catholic pressure. As it happened, this conclusion may not have been off the mark. Shortly afterwards, Senator Joseph Tydings of Maryland reported at a Department of Health, Education & Welfare conference that "HEW departmental spokesmen advised that no new Federal funds would be available." And Dr. Eugene Guthrie, Associate Surgeon General of the Public Health Service, stated, "We just couldn't get the money for family planning programs."

Fearing such reaction against governmental support, the Fund immediately prepared an ad to answer the Bishops' attack. Headlined "Catholic Bishops Assail Birth Control As Millions Face Starvation," the ad declared that with India and other nations on the brink of starvation, disaster could only by averted by in-

NATIONAL COUNCIL OF THE CHURCHES OF CHRIST IN THE UNITED STATES OF AMERICA

CHURCH WORLD SERVIC

475 RIVERSIDE DRIVE • NEW YORK, N. Y. 10027

Cable: DOMINI

April 1, 1966

Church World Service Department
James MacCracken
Executive Director

Mr. Hugh Moore
Hugh Moore Fund
60 East 42nd Street
New York, New York 10017

Dear Mr. Moore:

I doubt you could do a more important bit of work than to stimulate the interest of the American public in doing something about this most gigantic of all world problems. Your "Famine stalks the Earth" ads are most compelling and informative. We who are in the business of applying the voluntarily given resources of our people to projects for meeting the root causes of hunger, as well as to emergency feeding programs, do salute you!

You are undoubtedly aware of the National Council of Churches' Resolution on World Hunger, and, therefore, know of our increased emphasis in this area of the churches' concern. In case you have not seem a copy of this resolution, we have enclosed one for your information.

Mr. Vernon Trudo has asked your office to send reprints of your advertisement. We will distribute these to our constituency as supplementary interpretation material. We would plan to send the reprint to councils of churches, ministerial associations, and community churches. We would also make its availability known to the interpretation people in our member denominations as some of them might wish to make use of additional reprints.

Sincerely yours,

James MacCracken
Executive Director
Church World Service Department

JM:ms
cc: Mr. Vernon Trudo

A Program of the Division of Overseas Ministries

creased Federal commitment. "Without population control," it concluded, "the Food for Peace program will be a mere stopgap, saving the lives of those who would produce still more hungry people."

Because the ad openly criticized the Catholic hierarchy for the first time, the Fund sought widespread support from other religious denominations. In addition to an impressive list of businessmen, statesmen, scientists, and authors, the signers included the Rt. Rev. Stephen Bayne, vice president, executive council, the Episcopal Church; the Rt. Rev. Henry Knox Sherrill, former president, World Council of Churches; Bishop A. Raymond Grant of the Methodist Church, and Rabbi Maurice N. Eisendrath, president, Union of American Hebrew Congregations.

Not only was the ad controversial among the general public, but it received unenthusiastic reactions among some elements of the population movement. As with the Fund's first publications in 1954, the ad was labelled "reckless" and "inflammatory." The spirit of ecumenism had convinced some birth control leaders that the Catholic hierarchy must be pacified rather than confronted boldly.

"But Hugh Moore always had the courage to call a spade a spade, the strength to stand up and say the Catholic hierarchy was wrong," Elmo Roper has argued. "You need that kind of man out front."

"He was the only person I ever knew who brought the Catholic Church face to face with one of its greatest dilemmas," said another of his supporters.

The Fund not only placed the ad in *The New York Times* and *The Washington Post,* but it was determined to reach as many liberal Catholics as possible by taking prominent space in *The National Catholic Reporter* and *Commonweal* magazine. Then it booked a two-page spread in *Time* and *Harper's* magazines to complete the Fund's most ambitious campaign up to that time.

Asked why the Fund should continue to devote its modest resources to advertising year after year when the population movement seemed to be making progress, Moore liked to tell the story of William Wrigley, founder of the chewing gum company, who was riding with a friend from Chicago to New York on the Twentieth Century Limited. Why didn't Wrigley reduce his advertising and increase his profits? the friend asked. "The Century is going more than 75 miles an hour right now," Wrigley retorted. "Why not take off the locomotive?"

Advertising's Secondary Audience

The impact of the Bishops ad on reader opinion was only the beginning of its influence. As a result of thousands of coupon requests, the ad reached a widening circle of local community groups.

Professors who wanted the ad for classroom reading and ministers who distributed it to their parishioners often requested 500 to 1,000 copies. The surprising reaction was the number of favorable Catholic responses.

One Catholic housewife in Connecticut, asking 100 copies for her Catholic friends, informed her parish priest she would no longer support the church until the hierarchy's position on birth control had changed.

A Catholic student at a California university requested 500 copies to distribute at the opening of a Catholic student center where bishops and other church officials would be present.

Another Catholic student at a Wisconsin university tacked the ad to his dormitory bulletin board with a petition requesting Wisconsin Congressmen to support population programs. Almost 50 students signed the petition, many listing themselves as Catholics.

Professors at many Catholic colleges, including the University of Notre Dame, requested copies. All told, over 75,000 reprints of the Bishops ad were distributed by the Fund.

In addition to these coupon requests, the Fund launched 12

different mail campaigns based on the same advertisement. One large mailing went to a selected list of Protestant and Jewish clergymen particularly involved in social action and international affairs.

Because the Fund wanted the message to reach all government officials who might affect population policies, another mailing went to the secretaries of all executive departments, 300 Washington bureau officials, and members of the White House staff. A similar letter went to hundreds of hospital and public health officials in every state and major city.

Inasmuch as the United Nations was deeply concerned with world population policy, the Fund sent personal letters with the ad to all ambassadors at the UN and chiefs of missions, to all key officers at the United Nations Educational Scientific and Cultural Organization (UNESCO), United Nations Children's Fund (UNICEF), the Food and Agriculture Organization and the World Health Organization.

The Fund directed another mailing to hundreds of national organizations concentrating on peace, population and international affairs.

To stimulate press coverage, the Fund sent a special letter with the ad to hundreds of editorial writers at leading papers throughout the country, to columnists and religious editors. One mailing was aimed specifically at Catholic magazines and newspapers.

In this same period of the Bishops ad campaign, the Fund also directed a massive mailing at the nation's "thought leaders." Moore believed that government population programs could be achieved best by winning over clergymen, lawyers, doctors, educators, businessmen and other leaders who had gained the eminence of inclusion in *Who's Who*. Such campaigns on a smaller scale had produced striking results in previous years. Now the Fund did a personalized mailing to 80,000 people selected from *Who's Who in America*, *Who's Who of American Women* and *The American Catholic Who's Who*—a mailing that contributed to further pressure on Washington.

Controversy—and Catalysis

If Hugh Moore ranks as the fiery controversialist of the population movement, he was also one of its chief catalysts for decades, serving on the boards of most of the private organizations in the field. He built some organizations from the idea stage. Others he supported in trouble and nursed to vigorous health. "He always comes up with the essential idea at the right time," General Draper has pointed out. "He knows whom to consult to get an idea into shape. He works over an idea relentlessly. But once he decides to move, he moves fast."

"He has an amazing ability to activate others by putting over the tremendous urgency of his idea," said a nationally known publicist. "Doggedly persistent, he just refuses to give up."

A prime example of this determination was the population conference at Columbia University's American Assembly, which has long had the reputation of bringing together the best minds in the nation on key public issues. In 1955, Moore first talked to

CLIFFORD C. NELSON, President of Columbia University's American Assembly.

Dr. Henry M. Wriston, the Assembly's director, and urged him to make population the subject of a four-day conference at Arden House. But Wriston contended that the Assembly had a long list of issues taking precedence. Moore hammered away at him year after year, finally asking Marriner Eccles, an Assembly trustee, to take over the campaign.

Finally in 1963 the University asked Moore to help in organizing an Assembly on population. His rejoinder was, "I shall indeed be glad to do it, but I should remind you that there are 300 million more people in the world to worry about than there were when I first approached you."

The leading authorities on population met at Arden House and concluded that "time is running out for the formulation and implementation of a world and a national population policy."

If Moore had the foresight to build an essential organization, he also had the courage to leave it after completing his mission. "He put every moment for two years into the Emergency Campaign," Mrs. Robert Ferguson, a veteran leader of the movement, recalled. "But when the time seemed right to combine it with Planned Parenthood, he had no regrets, no resentment. He just said to Planned Parenthood, 'It's your baby,' and went to his next objective."

Through the years, however, Moore continued financial support of Planned Parenthood—World Population, a support that its chief executive, former Congressman Paul H. Todd, Jr., graciously acknowledged in 1969 with these words: "Coming from a man who has exerted such influence on the birth control movement for as long as you have, [your aid] is doubly welcome. The time, effort and intelligence you have expended on behalf of the people less fortunate than yourself is the beacon that the rest of us can guide our lives by."

In 1954, Guy Irving Burch, a prominent demographer who headed the Population Reference Bureau in Washington, told Moore the Bureau had exhausted its finances. Moore considered the Bureau essential for its authoritative, scientific reports, widely

used by educational institutions, newspapers, and other information media. He agreed to support the Bureau, and set about first
to meet and then enlarge the Bureau's miniscule budget. After
Burch died, Robert and Annabelle Cook took over its direction.
As board chairman, Moore enlisted as trustees a distinguished
group of businessmen, including Frank Abrams of Jersey Standard; Walter Bergman, president of Lily-Tulip Cup Company; and
Lawrence Wilkinson, executive vice president of Continental Can
Company.

Through Abrams and other directors, who had strong links to
the major foundations, the Bureau secured sizable grants from
Ford, Rockefeller and The Population Council. Moore also advanced "seed money" through which it could embark on public
fund-raising campaigns. "He gave you the tools with which you
could take off," Annabelle Cook has recalled. By 1966, Moore had
helped raise the Bureau's annual budget to $400,000.

Today, the Bureau's *Population Bulletin* has become the source
of at least 5,000 newspaper stories annually. The product of in-
tensive research, its articles present a humanized approach to
population—"Spotlight on Marriage" which revealed the dangers
of early U.S. marriages and the bunching of births within a few
years after marriage; "One Man's Family," the story of a farmer
with 410 descendants and what happens when a family multiplies
beyond its resources. At the same time, *Bulletin* articles are fre-
quently ahead of the headlines. "Water Shortages in the United
States" appeared long before the crisis of the sixties; "Algeria:
Peace and Human Arithmetic" during that nation's struggle for
independence.

With a new branch office in Bogota, Colombia, the Bureau now
distributes its publications in Spanish throughout Latin America
and has tapped a rising demand for population information among
newspapers and government agencies. Some of its publications
were made official documents at the 1967 meeting of the Organization of American States in Caracas. "I have seen the Bureau
grow from a one-man operation to a national organization of

stature and influence," Moore wrote. After ten years as board chairman, he considered his objectives accomplished, resigned in 1967, and was elected honorary chairman by his fellow trustees.

A significant detail in Hugh Moore's campaign to lure prestigious businessmen to positions on these boards was his decisive grip on all meetings. "He promised me that every luncheon meeting would begin at 12:15 and end on the dot of 2:15," Frederick Osborn recalled. "He has never yet broken this promise."

Mentioning the Unmentionable

His friends were somewhat appalled, however, when he became president of the Association for Voluntary Sterilization in 1964. Sterilization was the abandoned stepchild of the population movement. In the popular mind, it was still connected with surgery on imbeciles, with castration, and even with the horrors of Nazi concentration camps.

DR. BROCK CHISHOLM, former head of the World Health Organization and Honorary Chairman of the Association for Voluntary Sterilization, Inc.

ARTHUR GODFREY at the 1969 conference of the Association for Voluntary Sterilization, Inc. Hugh Moore, the organization's Chairman, has just completed his speech to the conference.

The early advocates of voluntary sterilization considered such criticism valid enough to believe they must hide their identity under the vague title of "The Human Betterment Association." One of Moore's first objectives was to insist the organization state its purpose boldly and change its name to the Association for Voluntary Sterilization.

Following his tested pattern, he brought such eminent persons as Dr. Brock Chisholm, first director-general of the World Health Organization, onto the Board. He raised money to move the office to a midtown New York suite just off Fifth Avenue, and employed an experienced executive director and staff. Since the principal obstacle to sterilization was lack of public understanding of its legality and medical acceptance, the Association appointed Dr. H. Curtis Wood, Jr., a Philadelphia obstetrician, as medical director. Crisscrossing the country on speaking tours, Wood made as many as 110 lectures and radio and television appearances a year. As public acceptance increased nearly 200,000 Americans annually chose this method of birth control.

The Association for Voluntary Sterilization aggressively challenged the prejudices of Federal and local governments on sterilization. When the Office of Economic Opportunity prohibited sterilization in its welfare clinics program, though its Congressional mandate sanctioned "birth control," the Association insisted the procedure should be treated as an acceptable form of birth control. When Connecticut, one of only two states then requiring medical indication for sterilization, prohibited the procedure in its welfare program, the Association attacked the decision as religious bigotry. By the end of 1966, both the Department of Defense and Department of Health, Education & Welfare announced their support of sterilization as a form of family planning. Two years later the Planned Parenthood Federation finally approved sterilization.

The chief psychological block remained the assumed finality of surgery. Moore and his associates decided to encourage scientific research to produce a reversible technique. Because male steriliza-

DR. JOHN K. LATTIMER, Professor of Urology at Columbia University's College of Physicians and Surgeons. He has devoted his considerable talents to the search for better methods of male contraception.

DR. SRIPATI CHANDRASEKHAR, Minister of Health and Family Planning in the Government of India, one of the most eloquent advocates of population control in Asia.

tion, or vasectomy, lent itself best to reversibility, he gave financial support to experiments based on closing the seminal tubes with a plastic clip. When this showed little promise, he convinced the Rockefeller Foundation to finance new approaches by Dr. John Lattimer, one of the nation's leading urologists, at the Columbia College of Physicians and Surgeons.

In 1968, on behalf of the Association for Voluntary Sterilization, Moore invited Dr. S. Chandrasekhar, whom he first met in New Delhi in 1959, to come to the United States. Chandrasekhar had become Minister of State for Health and Family Planning in the Indian cabinet. The Minister accepted the invitation and made numerous speeches around the country stating that sterilization is India's best hope. He agreed while in the U.S. to accept the chairmanship of an international association for voluntary sterilization.

"Fire Power" in Washington

It had become Hugh Moore's ever-increasing conviction that the only hope of solving the population problem in time lay in the most massive U.S. Government financing for research, education, and training in the field, both at home and abroad. The need for money was so great that it was already beyond the scope of any and all private foundation efforts. So he began thinking in terms of an additional organization designed specifically to bring greater government involvement and working right at the seat of power in Washington—the organization soon to be called the Population Crisis Committee.

Moore's conception of the PCC epitomizes what General Draper had called "the essential idea at the right time." Despite the Hugh Moore Fund's advertising and mail campaigns directed at the government, the population movement still lacked "real fire power" in Washington. "None of our projects brought the necessary sense of urgency," Moore told an associate. "We just didn't have the necessary impact on the government."

What he visualized was a select committee—its name carefully fashioned to convey urgency—to be headed by a nationally-recognized figure with unchallenged respect in the government. After meeting with Draper and Cass Canfield, chairman of the governing body of the International Planned Parenthood Federation and getting their support, he pushed ahead with plans for a fundraising dinner, which collected the necessary $100,000, and lined up an eminent board of directors.

For national chairman, he thought of Senator Kenneth Keating of New York, who had just lost his seat to Robert F. Kennedy after a distinguished career. Moore had never met Keating, and the Senator was known to be considering a dozen lucrative offers that would pay him many times what the Population Crisis Committee could afford. Moore arranged a luncheon at New York's Century Club, however, and, in three hours of relentless persuasion, convinced Keating that he was the man for the job. A few weeks later Elmo Roper met Keating at the house of a mutual friend and asked what made him accept. "You know Hugh Moore," Keating laughed, "How can anyone say no to him?"

"Your first impression of him is that he's a man with a mission," Keating later recalled. "He's a forceful man whose enthusiasm rubs off on everyone around him."

Keating opened an office in Washington, and soon became what an associate called "the first popular spokesman for population control in the United States." In addition to speeches across the country, his great contribution was personal contacts in the Executive Branch. He ate in the private Senate dining room where he could spread the gospel of family planning among old friends, particularly among the Republican leadership. As one of them recalled, "We may have kidded Ken at first, telling him that he should go and talk to so-and-so whose wife had just had another baby. But his persuasiveness paid off, and he was able to give respectability to these discussions on population."

In the fall of 1965, Keating accepted the nomination of the Republican Party for the New York Court of Appeals, that state's

CASS CANFIELD, head of Harper & Row, a director of the Population Crisis Committee and Chairman of the Governing Body of the International Planned Parenthood Federation.

Paul Wilkes

KENNETH B. KEATING, former U.S. Senator and first National Chairman of the Population Crisis Committee.

highest tribunal, and won the election handily. After several years on the bench, Keating went on to become the U.S. Ambassador to India. Writing the Hugh Moore Fund somewhat later from New Delhi, Keating remarked: "As first chairman of the Population Crisis Committee, I first became aware of the ominous statistical dimensions of the population problem. But it was not until my arrival in India, and particularly my first visit to Calcutta, that I felt the impact of the awful human misery resulting from overpopulation."

With Keating's 1965 departure from PCC, Moore, who had earlier seen India's misery at first hand and deeply felt the urgency it lent to the cause, set out to seek another national chairman. "I was afraid the Population Crisis Committee was washed up without a man of stature equal to Keating's," he admitted. "Then I looked around and realized that General Draper was an ideal choice."

Draper lived in California. He would have to give up a sumptuous home in Palo Alto and move to Washington. "My assumption in our talks was that he was so dedicated to the importance of this cause that he would devote the rest of his life to it," Moore has recalled. After discussing the matter with Mrs. Draper, the General not only accepted the post but insisted on working without compensation—even using his own funds.

An intense, driving man with wide contacts at the highest government levels, Draper made PCC a powerful force in Washington. He initiated a series of luncheon meetings at which Congressmen and government leaders not only had the chance to discuss the population problem with each other but hear the latest reports from experts like Dr. Jack Lippes, developer of the intra-uterine device, and Dr. Sheldon Segal, director of The Population Council's biomedical division. Special briefings were held for the State Department staff with panels of experts. One conference focused on the teaching of reproductive biology at Catholic medical schools; another on the relationship of family planning and mental health.

WILLIAM S. GAUD, Administrator of the United States Agency for International Development, signs a contract with Gen. William H. Draper Jr. to provide government funds for the work of the International Planned Parenthood Federation.

Draper personally became the prime consultant on two crucial pieces of population legislation—Senator J. William Fulbright's bill to appropriate $150 million over three years for family planning abroad, and Senator Joseph Tydings' bill to appropriate $230 million over five years for domestic family planning. Draper not only testified himself, but lined up imposing experts to appear before Congressional committees and kept Congressmen constantly supplied with reports and statistics on the population problem.

"I have gradually become convinced that unless and until the population explosion now erupting in Asia, Africa and Latin America is brought under control, our entire economic program is doomed to failure," Draper told the Foreign Affairs Committee.

"Our basic and very worthy objective is to help the poor nations of the world in their efforts to raise their per capita standard of living so that their people can participate in at least some of the material blessings we now enjoy. Unfortunately this is proving to be impossible. Rapid population growth is offsetting increased economic resources almost everywhere. Failure to satisfy the revolution of rising expectations is already sowing the seeds of discontent in many countries. I believe that our own government, in the cause of humanity and its own enlightened self-interest, should accord the highest priority to the world population problem and emphasize this priority throughout our foreign aid program."

"Draper really went out and rang the alarm bell in Washington," said a prominent government official commenting on the General's five years as head of the Population Crisis Committee.

Hugh Moore agreed, and, upon Draper's retirement from PCC in 1969, he took the lead in arranging a testimonial dinner at Washington's Shoreham Hotel attended by some 400 notables. With Cass Canfield and Elmo Roper as his co-hosts, Moore paid tribute to Draper's work for population control in the high echelons of the U.S. Government and around the world. Other speakers at the dinner, which Draper himself made newsworthy

GENERAL WILLIAM H. DRAPER JR., retiring Chairman of the Population Crisis Committee, is presented with a clock by Hugh Moore, the organization's initiator, at a Washington dinner in Draper's honor, December 1969. John W. Snyder, former Secretary of the Treasury, at right.

by declaring PCC's goal to be zero population growth for the U.S. by the year 2000, included General Lucius Clay, John D. Rockefeller 3rd, Paul Hoffman, and, as toastmaster, former Postmaster General J. Edward Day.

The Quest for Peace

In almost two decades, Hugh Moore has never wavered from the concept that world peace depends on population control. This same singleness of purpose underlay his business career. That began in 1910 when he and a friend set about raising funds to start America's first paper drinking cup manufactury. By 1937, he had built the Dixie Cup Company into a prosperous corporation and had amassed enough money to fulfill his ambitions.* Yet his real work had only begun. As the threat of war from Nazi and Fascist dictatorships loomed over Europe, he who had served in the first World War, and whose two sons would serve in the second, became increasingly concerned about the role businessmen could play in world peace. "I thought if there was anything I could do so that my grandsons and their generation would not face a third World War, I should do it," he has recalled.

It was obvious that some form of international organization was a first requirement for world order. But it was not until the nineteen fifties that the population explosion loomed as a root cause of war and engaged Moore's attention.

In 1939, he had become chairman of the executive committee of the League of Nations Association, which advocated U.S. entry into the League. When Germany invaded Poland, Moore became convinced that the best protection for the United States was aid to Britain, then restricted by our Neurality Act. As co-founder of the Committee to Defend America by Aiding the Allies, and chairman of its executive committee, he collaborated with William

---

* For more about Moore's business career, please see Appendix.

Allen White, the national chairman and noted Kansas publisher, to put together an illustrious list of sponsors including Lewis W. Douglas, Thomas K. Finletter, James W. Gerard, Thomas Lamont and Robert E. Sherwood. With 50 chapters around the country, the committee soon became a significant national force.

As a spokesman for peace, Moore was appointed by the National Peace Conference, made up of 40 American peace organizations, to go to Washington to meet with President Roosevelt. The purpose was to get the President to call a conference of Western nations to avert the impending war.

He had been warned that Roosevelt could be supremely loquacious, that he once talked to a delegate about rhododendrons for 20 minutes without letting the visitors get in a word about their purpose.

> "I made up my mind," Moore recalls "that I couldn't be decapitated if I interrupted the President. I presented our plan. He interrupted. I interrupted him. At the end of 20 minutes, a secretary appeared but Roosevelt ignored him. We talked another 20 minutes. The secretary tried to stop the conversation again, and we talked for a final 20 minutes. 'Hitler has already told me in effect to go to hell,' said the President at one point—and did not summon the meeting of heads of state requested by the National Peace Conference."

As World War II drew to a close, Moore intensified his work for world peace. With money he had made from Dixie cups he set up the Hugh Moore Fund in 1944 as a non-profit educational foundation to promote peace. In the same year he and his associates foresaw the need of well thought-out plans for a new world peace-keeping organization. They formed a group which came to be known as Americans United for World Organization. Dr. Ernest M. Hopkins, president of Dartmouth College, was elected chairman; Moore, president. Wendell Willkie, defeated Republican candidate for President in 1940, now at the peak of his popularity, worked ceaselessly in support of the committee. When the historic conference to establish the United Nations was held in San Francisco in 1945, the State Department appointed a number of consultants to the U.S. delegation, including Moore. Each morning these consultants met with Secretary of State Edward Stettinius, analyzing the proceedings of the previous day, helping to mold the eventual UN charter.

In 1947, when Secretary of State George C. Marshall proposed his plan of economic aid to save Europe from collapse, it was considered essential to rally the widest possible public support. Former Secretary of War Henry L. Stimson organized a nucleus of leaders, including Dean Acheson and Robert Patterson, and launched the Committee for the Marshall Plan. With Moore as treasurer, the Committee opened offices in New York and Washington, started a campaign of speeches throughout the country, and maintained strong pressure on Congress until the plan was enacted into law.

Steps Toward Atlantic Unity

Increasingly, Hugh Moore's efforts were concentrated on organizational techniques for world peace. With the formation of the North Atlantic Treaty Organization, Justice Owen J. Roberts, recently resigned from the U.S. Supreme Court, and former Under Secretary of State Will Clayton, realizing that military alliances do not last, organized a movement in 1949 to promote a federal union of the democracies. Moore, who became chairman of the executive committee, described its objectives: "The strength of the free world resided in Atlantic countries on both sides of the ocean. It was the theory of the Atlantic Union Committee that if peace was to be secured, it would reside in those nations. What we wished was a form of union like the U.S. federal union through which the Western nations could act as a group rather than as competitors."

Atlantic Union's first significant support came in 1954 when

ELMO ROPER, famed public opinion analyst, Vice Chairman of the Population Crisis Committee and a vigorous advocate of population control.

Fabian Bachrach

Prime Minister Louis St. Laurent of Canada advocated "closer integration . . . within the larger framework of the North Atlantic community." After his speech, a committee including Elmo Roper, Philip D. Reed, Walden Moore, William Draper and Hugh Moore drafted a Declaration of Atlantic Unity. The declaration was then signed by 244 Western leaders whom *The New York Times* called the most distinguished group ever to endorse an international document.

After long pressure by the Atlantic Union Committee, the U.S. Senate's Foreign Relations Committee held hearings on a resolution for an exploratory convention. The resolution failed, but Clayton, Roberts, Roper and Moore, who had become chairman of the group's executive committee, determinedly presented it again and again for a decade. "You have no idea what it has meant to me," Justice Roberts wrote Moore, "to have so able and prudent a man at the helm."

In January 1962, an unprecedented convention was held in Paris. Delegates from 14 nations, including Britain's Sir John

UNITED STATES COMMISSIONERS to the Atlantic Convention with Christian B. Herter, former U.S. Secretary of State (left of flag), as their chairman. The purpose of the convention, held in Paris in 1962, was to consider more effective means of cooperation among the members of the North Atlantic Treaty Organization, all of which were represented at the meeting. The "Declaration of Paris," which was adopted after some weeks of discussion, included a clause, introduced by Hugh Moore (center of front row), recognizing the urgency of the population problem.

Slessor, Marshal of the Air Force, Christian Herter, former U.S. Secretary of State, and Paul Van Zeeland, former Prime Minister of Belgium, met to discuss the North Atlantic Alliance and recommend measures to strengthen it economically and politically. Moore, as one of the 20 officially appointed U.S. representatives concentrated on swinging delegates to a population plank. As a result, the final text of the Declaration of Paris included the significant injunction:

"That, in view of the hundreds of millions of hungry people alive today and the prospect that there will be three billion more persons in the next generation, the Atlantic Community be requested to address itself forthwith to the population problem."

In the postwar period Moore worked with almost every American group seeking means to stabilize the world—the American Association for the United Nations, the Commission to Study the Organization of Peace, the Council on Foreign Relations. By Congressional appointment, he became a member of the Commission on NATO. Woodrow Wilson, creator of the League of Nations, had been Moore's youthful idol, so Moore happily accepted two five-year terms as a member of the executive committee and chairman of the finance committee of the Woodrow Wilson Foundation.

"I have been eminently fortunate to work with the two greatest women of our time, Mrs. Sanger and Mrs. Eleanor Roosevelt," he once recalled. "Mrs. Roosevelt and I were fellow board members in the American Association for the United Nations, meeting together weekly for a lengthy period. One day she said to me she was afraid she would have to miss the next meeting. She was going around the world, she said—the trip that included her notable visit to Egypt where she walked fearlessly through angry crowds demonstrating against the United States. That was the only meeting she ever missed."

Bradford F. Herzog

DR. JOHN CRAYTON SNYDER, Dean of the Harvard School of Public
Health, greeting Mr. and Mrs. Hugh Moore at the Population Center of the
school in Boston in 1969. Moore is a member of the school's Visiting
Committee.

Business and Population

Hugh Moore was becoming so absorbed in his quasi-public pursuits that he divided his time between New York and Easton, Pennsylvania, headquarters of the Dixie Cup Company. In Pennsylvania he lived in a Pennsylvania Dutch house of gray stone on 120 rolling acres of farmland. In New York, he kept a permanent apartment at an East Side hotel near his office.

Moore's energy continued to appall his associates. His hair, although grayed, kept its brown cast. His mustache, always neatly trimmed, was almost dapper. He bounded along New York's crowded streets, taking taxis only for long distances. Often his New York schedule started with an appointment at 9:30 a.m. and continued through lunch and dinner meetings until 10 at night. In Pennsylvania he usually got to his office by 8 a.m., worked till noon, then went home for lunch and continued work in the isolated tower study of his house. Until a blood clot in his leg placed him under a strict medical regimen, he commuted from Easton to New York by public bus. He then made the concession of using his own chauffeured car.

Although the Hugh Moore Fund consistently emphasized "action" projects directed at the government, some aspects of its work touched broader areas of public information. It regularly sent copies of the *Population Bomb* pamphlet to libraries, colleges and other information centers. The Fund made grants to foreign policy groups, enabling a specific magazine issue or report on population to reach a wider audience among colleges or schools. Its staff worked closely with magazines and radio and television producers in developing articles and programs on population. Sometimes the Fund made grants to publishers to help significant population books. It also lent its name to, and aided distribution of, such a landmark volume as Paul Ehrlich's *The Population Bomb*. Finally, it ran its own news service—a pamphlet of four-to-eight pages with important population clippings from the press, known as *Population Bomb Press Clippings* and distributed quarterly to a selected mailing list.

Population Bomb Press Clippings, at first called *News Items*, is published from time to time by the Hugh Moore Fund. Started in 1963, it now goes free to some 12,000 persons and institutions that request it.

SIR GRANTLEY ADAMS, Prime Minister of the British West Indian Federation, receives an award from the Hugh Moore Fund. Sir Grantley was the first politician known to run for office on a birth control program.

In 1968, Harvard's President Pusey invited Moore to become a member of the Visiting Committee of the School of Public Health which had established a Center for Population Studies. The Fund has made grants to the Center and to population forums at Lafayette College and Boston University. It gave an award for distinguished service in population control to Sir Grantley H. Adams, first President of the British West Indies Federation.

From the earliest days of the Fund, Moore not only involved businessmen such as Lammot duPont Copeland of the DuPont Company but urged the business community to take a vigorous role in population control. The myth persisted, however, that more people meant more business. As late as 1966, an editorial in one of the trade magazines for toymakers attacked the birth control movement for damaging its potential market. "It isn't the number of people that counts," said Moore in a pamphlet rebutting this theory, "but *purchasing power*, which is higher in an economy with a stabilized population."

By 1960, when Moore helped to organize the Margaret Sanger dinner at the Waldorf-Astoria, he was convinced that the time had come for a direct campaign among businessmen. Marriner S. Eccles, a member of the Population Policy Panel of the Hugh Moore Fund and former head of the Federal Reserve System, was invited to give one of the principal addresses. "With a continuation of the present population growth," Eccles said, "many American communities will find themselves in serious financial difficulties." While population increased 18 percent from 1950 to 1960, expenditures in state and local government soared 110 percent. "Our total tax load as a percentage of our national income is likely to increase unless there is a drastic reduction in our rate of population growth," Eccles concluded. "Our entire concept of a healthy and happy world at peace, with pestilence and premature death eradicated, is totally unrealistic unless we recognize the severe limitations of population growth which are necessary in the United States as well as the rest of the world."

The speech had an important impact in business circles. How-

MARRINER S. ECCLES, former Chairman of the Federal Reserve Board and member of the World Population Emergency Campaign organized by the Hugh Moore Fund.

ever, Moore has recalled that "a noted demographer said to me afterward, 'I can never forgive you for having given time to such an inflammatory speech.' I replied, 'You've been raised in academic halls. I've been raised in the market place. I'm used to presenting facts dramatically. Students of demography have talked for years and nobody listened. But that speech was quoted throughout the country, and got the attention of thousands of people who had never thought of the population problem before.' "

The Case For Speaking Out

Moore's shock tactics to get the business community into the population movement, particularly his disagreement with the Catholic Church, worried many birth control leaders at the time.

"A decade ago, most businessmen not only ignored the

HUGH and LOUISE MOORE at the 8th International Conference on Family Planning of the International Planned Parenthood Federation in Santiago, Chile, in 1967.

ROBERT B. FISKE, corporation executive, who organized the world meeting of the International Planned Parenthood Federation at Santiago, Chile, in 1967. It was attended by representatives of 84 nations.

population problem but were afraid of their Catholic customers," he said. "A few like Copeland of the DuPont Company were in a rare position. They could speak out without fear of their jobs. I think this fear was exaggerated. I remember the president of a large corporation telling me he wanted to sign one of our ads but his advisers opposed it. Later he wrote that they had been wrong—that he should have gone ahead.

"My outspoken position never affected Dixie cup sales. No pressure was ever brought by Catholic groups to my knowledge. When I first started mailing out *The Population Bomb,* however, I would get letters from Catholics saying it was too bad my mother didn't know about birth control before I was born. But that reaction has practically disappeared. We rarely get a letter of protest today. In my trip to the International Planned Parenthood conference at Santiago, Chile, in 1967, the most impressive fact was that the Catholic President of Chile *opened* the conference and that many priests and Catholic officials took part in it.

"A number of the population leaders insisted from the beginning that the Catholic Church would go along if we spoke softly about birth control. I felt that the Church would never compromise until it lost communicants over the issue. The day has arrived when young couples go to their confessor and he has no satisfactory solution for their problem. They do not go back, and this has led to a breach between parishioners and hierarchy. The Church has never softened its position on contraceptives, whereas most of its parishioners either use them or approve of their use."

Moore's shrewd sense of timing convinced him by 1962 that conditions were ripe for a Congressional committee to tackle the population control problem. He consulted his Congressman, Francis E. Walter of Pennsylvania, chairman of a subcommittee of the House Committee on the Judiciary. Walter's specialization had long been immigration policy. Moore persuaded him that immigration must be studied against the whole population crisis and that hearings should look into "the relationship between the growth of our population, the problems of automation, unemployment and partial employment, and the shift of population from rural to urban areas." (The subcommittee ultimately used these words in its final report.)

Working closely with the committee, Moore helped to assemble the first notable array of population experts to testify before a government body. Their vivid reports made a deep impression on the Congressmen of the committee and brought nation-wide press coverage. Dr. Philip Hauser, chairman of the University of Chicago's department of sociology, for example, concluded: "Contemporary rates of population growth make the prospect of raising world productivity, and thereby the average world level of living, a dim one indeed. The present rate of world population increase cannot possibly persist for very long into the future."

The pattern set by the Walter subcommittee was followed and

DR. PHILIP M. HAUSER, Professor of Sociology at the University of Chicago, for years in the front rank of exponents of population control. As a speaker he has had few equals in the field.

Corona Studios

enlarged a few years later by the exhaustive hearings held by Senator Ernest Gruening. Calling over a hundred prominent witnesses, the Gruening hearings filled a dozen volumes—the ultimate compendium of knowledge on the population crisis.

The Campaign to Check the Population Explosion

By late 1967, most Americans had already heard of the population explosion. There had been mounting publicity, resulting from the bulletins of the Population Reference Bureau, the releases of the Planned Parenthood Federation, and the controversy with the Catholic hierarchy. The Federal Government had increased its appropriations for birth control by a modest amount and private citizens had subscribed some millions of dollars to be sent abroad to the fledgling units of International Planned Parenthood in the underdeveloped countries. People spoke optimistically of the "progress being made."

But the fact was that world population, which had been 2½ billion in 1953 increased in 15 short years to 3½ billion by 1968. In 1953, the annual increase was 35 million; by 1968 it was double that, namely 70 million persons a year.

The American people generally were not worried about the population problem. The Federal expenditure for "family planning, domestic and international," was less ($29.2 million in fiscal 1967) than that expended for a hundred less important problems. Private health organizations—cancer, heart, and TB—had many times more money for education and promotion than the population movement.

In view of this situation, Moore embarked upon one of the most ambitious projects of his life. He invited a small group to lunch at the Century Club in New York to see what could be done to arouse the public and the government to raise their sights and get action commensurate with the magnitude of the problem.

He proposed that the government set up a "Manhattan Project" for population control—an allusion to the giant crash project that developed the atomic bomb so quickly during World War II.

At the luncheon were Emerson Foote and Henry C. Flower, Jr., two of the nation's leading advertising authorities; Elmo Roper, public opinion analyst; Harold Bostrom, a prominent industrialist; Rockefeller Prentice, philanthropist; Adolph Schmidt, foundation executive with the Mellon interests, in addition to General Draper and Moore. "The time has come," Moore said, "for top leaders in public relations and advertising to become involved with the population problem." After considerable discussion, which continued through several subsequent meetings at the Century, the group agreed to go ahead as an *ad hoc* committee of the Hugh Moore Fund, to be known as the Campaign to Check the Population Explosion.

Mr. Foote consented to go into the office of the Fund and direct the Campaign as chairman, without compensation. A budget of

HAROLD BOSTROM, a Wisconsin businessman who dedicated a part of his substantial fortune to the advancement of the birth control movement, and was an initiator of the first national Congress on Optimum Population and Environment in June 1970.

EMERSON FOOTE, leading advertising man and Chairman of the widely-known Campaign to Check the Population Explosion, a committee of the Hugh Moore Fund.

Blackstone-Shelburne, N.Y.

THE NEW YORK TIMES

Pope denounces birth control as millions starve

BLACK STAR PHOTO

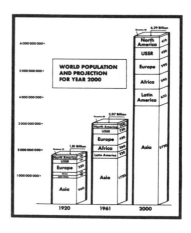

WORLD POPULATION AND PROJECTION FOR YEAR 2000

"Every marriage act must remain open to the transmission of life," said Pope Paul in his recent encyclical. He ruled out every action which proposes "to render procreation impossible."

The Pope denounced artificial contraception — the only practical means of controlling population. He held that it is not reasonable "to have recourse to artificial birth control" even though "we secure the harmony and peace of the family, and better conditions for the education of the children already born."

By his edict the Pope has struck a crushing blow against current efforts to reduce the flood of people now engulfing the earth.

In the advanced countries most couples—Catholics as well as Protestants—already practice birth control. But in the under-developed countries, such as in Latin America, the Pope's teaching may result in the birth of hordes of children who will not have enough to eat.

Famine already stalks the earth. Half of humanity goes to bed hungry every night. Ten thousand or more people are dying of starvation every day. This means that more than three and a half million starve to death every year. (The present tragic Biafra toll is *in addition* to these figures.)

As recently as 1953 there were 2½ billion people on earth. Today only 15 years later there are 3½ *billion*. A generation from now that number will approximately double at the present rate of increase, as the chart shows.

The Pope dismissed the population explosion with a few brief words, merely saying that it should be met by greater social and economic progress, rather than to resort to "utterly materialistic" measures to limit births.

The encyclical appears to millions of Catholics and Protestants as a rather incredible document, considering the eminence of the author and his access to the world's leading demographic, agricultural and other authorities. It is viewed by many as one of the most fateful blunders of modern times.

For there can be no doubt that unless population is brought under control at an early date the resulting human misery and social tensions will inevitably lead to chaos and strife—to revolutions and wars, the dimensions of which it would be hard to predict.

Nothing less than survival of the human race is at stake.

CAMPAIGN TO CHECK THE POPULATION EXPLOSION
EMERSON FOOTE, CHAIRMAN

$500,000 was pledged by the Fund and several other foundations and individuals.

As the program got under way late in 1967, full-page advertisements in leading newspapers and magazines were published to tell individual citizens what they could do, and urge the government to appropriate funds for a multibillion-dollar program of controlling the population explosion both at home and abroad.

The problem was treated in the advertising copy from a number of angles: overpopulation as a threat to peace, as a bringer of famines, as the cause of water and air pollution, as a breeder of crime, and as a dire effect of Pope Paul's edict against birth control. One of these advertisements won an accolade from the advertising profession, being cited as one of the year's ten best space ads by the leading trade journal *Advertising Age*. (Other examples of the advertisements are reproduced in the Appendix.)

Among the publications used were *The New York Times,* weekdays and Sunday editions, and *The Washington Post* and *The Washington Star* on a fairly regular basis; also *The Wall Street Journal, The Saturday Review, Esquire, Commonweal* and *The National Catholic Reporter.*

A distinguished group of individuals in all walks of American life agreed to sign the advertisements. These included Eugene R. Black, Dr. Detlev Bronk, Thomas D. Cabot, Dr. Philip M. Hauser, Rabbi Wolfe Kelman, Dr. Reinhold Niebuhr, Dr. Linus Pauling, Francis T. P. Plimpton, John Rock, M.D., Sidney A. Swensrud, and William H. Vanderbilt.

Thousands of replies were received from the public applauding the Campaign and requesting literature, offering assistance and ideas. They came from all over the country, from college professors, students, Protestant ministers, Jewish rabbis, church organizations and members of the general public.

Tens of thousands of reprints and pamphlets were mailed out in response to requests, government departments posted the ads in their offices. AID sent them to the U.S. missions overseas. Churches put them up on their bulletin boards. Students asked

DR. JOHN ROCK, famed co-devel-
oper of "the pill," a supporter of the
work of the Hugh Moore Fund.

for reprints in quantity to place in college libraries and dormi-
tories.

John Cowles, president of the Minneapolis *Star* and *Tribune,*
wrote, "Because I have been so favorably impressed by the effectiveness of the advertising campaign you are sponsoring to check
the population explosion, I would like to make ᴬt least a token
contribution to that cause."

Lewis Strauss, former head of the Atomic Energy Commission,
wrote, "The whole world is very much in your debt for the campaign in which you have been engaged and which, at long last,
seems to be making progress."

Marriner Eccles wrote, "I think you and your committee are
doing a whale of a job by the advertising campaign you are carrying on in so many important papers and publications."

President Johnson said that not nearly enough was being done
by government and appointed a high-level committee to make
recommendations.

The President Speaks

The advertising crusade continued over the Campaign's signature until its half-million-dollar war chest was exhausted in June 1969. By that time 19 different advertisements had appeared carrying the Campaign's name, for a total of 50-odd paid insertions and many free ones in space donated by friendly publishers or contributed by other interested persons or groups. Total circulation exceeded 40 million, with perhaps 140 million reader-exposures. Always, the media used were selected for their ability to reach the movers and shakers in Washington and in the business community.

Successful as the Campaign's program was during its early months, Hugh Moore felt still more had to be done quickly. Although President Kennedy had gone further than President Eisenhower, and President Johnson had gone beyond Kennedy with his appointment of a President's Committee on Population and Family Planning (Wilbur Cohen and John D. Rockefeller 3rd, co-chairmen), Moore felt that the government must put its full weight behind measures to stabilize population. Throughout its later advertising program, the Campaign bore down on this in its printed messages. Two full-page open letters were addressed to Richard M. Nixon, one just after his election in November 1968 and another soon after he took office. A double-page spread in *The New York Times* outlined the recommendations of the Johnson-appointed President's Committee, which had been made public a few days after Nixon's election.

When, in June 1969, the Campaign's funds were exhausted, Moore decided to ask his fellow directors of the Hugh Moore Fund to finance the advertising crusade alone. In late June another double-page advertisement appeared in *The Washington Post* and *The Washington Star*. This time the signature was the Hugh Moore Fund, but the style was that of the Campaign ads that had preceded it—large and forceful picture (a full-page portrait of World Bank President Robert McNamara), strong headlines, and hard-hitting copy based on a McNamara population

Anjan Gupta

HUGH MOORE and JOHN D. ROCKEFELLER 3rd at the Calcutta Airport in 1959 returning from the 6th International Conference on Family Planning of the International Planned Parenthood Federation.

RICHARD M. NIXON, who was the first American President to send a message to Congress recommending action to deal with the population problem.

speech (made even more potent by the dramatic fact that Mc-Namara's statement had been delivered to a Notre Dame University audience).

Mr. McNamara himself was quick to voice his approval of the endeavor. "I am convinced," he wrote to Hugh Moore, "that controlling population growth is a precondition of world progress. In bringing this issue to the attention of the public you are doing an important public service."

Within a month of the McNamara ad came the most far-reaching announcement the population movement had yet heard from an American President. In a message to Congress delivered July 18, 1969, President Nixon declared:

"Population growth is a world problem which no country can ignore.... The United Nations... and other international bodies should take leadership in responding to world population growth. The United States will cooperate fully.... In the United States... it would be unrealistic for the Federal Government alone to shoulder

Fabian Bachrach

ADOLPH W. SCHMIDT, United States Ambassador to Canada, formerly president of the A. W. Mellon Educational and Charitable Trust and a director of the Hugh Moore Fund. He brought large foundation resources to the aid of the population movement and was one of its most articulate spokesmen.

the entire burden, but this Administration does accept
a clear responsibility to provide essential leadership."
The President proposed another study commission but also directed several government agencies to step up population efforts
on which they were already engaged.

At about the same time, President Nixon appointed Adolph
W. Schmidt, a director of the Hugh Moore Fund, to be U.S.
Ambassador to Canada. Schmidt, formerly governor of T. Mellon
& Sons and a trustee of two Mellon foundations, foresaw potential
conflict between his foundation and government duties and so
reluctantly resigned from all the former.

"You know," he wrote Moore, "of my admiration and
approval of the pioneering work of the Hugh Moore Fund.
I think it has used its income and principal in the most
effective fashion possible, directed at the two most serious
and pressing problems of the world today, war prevention
and population growth stabilization. These are of necessity controversial fields, and your courage and good sense
in being willing to tackle them and find solutions deserves
the highest commendation."

New Goals Ahead

The first goal of Hugh Moore and his fellow campaigners had
been achieved. A President had accepted the responsibility of leading the nation to a responsible population policy. It was gratifying
to the 150 men and women who had been Moore's associates that
a letter soon arrived from the White House. Addressed to Moore,
it said in part, "We are very much aware of the fine public service
you have been engaged in through your advertising campaigns,
and believe that they have contributed a very great deal indeed
to increase public understanding of this critical problem." The
signature was that of Daniel P. Moynihan, special Assistant to the
President.

The White House letter also welcomed "any support that you

DANIEL P. MOYNIHAN, Presidential assistant, views the projected increase in U.S. population.

may wish to give the President's program"—a line of action that the Fund was already planning. A "merchandising" campaign parallelled publication of the ads in the newspapers. Soon after the McNamara ad appeared in the papers, for instance, 25,000 letters from the Fund went to selected lists of business executives, labor leaders, churchmen, journalists, educators, etc. Each enclosed the McNamara ad, offered reprint copies of it and copies of Mr. McNamara's full Notre Dame text. Immediately after the President's message, the letters were revised to urge that he be praised for what he had done—and asked to go further as fast as possible.

This became the theme of subsequent advertising. A double-spread advertisement in *The Times* and *The Washington Post* carried a full-page picture of the President and quoted his message in headline and text. It and subsequent ads offered free reprints of his Congressional message on population and urged the public to ask the President to implement his plans without delay. Some 85,000 copies of the message were distributed thus. President Nixon personally acknowledged the strength this lent his hand with the gracious letter of October 23, 1969, reproduced earlier in this volume.

"Whatever your cause, it's a lost cause," said the headline of another late-1969 ad, "unless we control population." This ran as a full page in *The New York Times* and later in *Fortune, Harper's, Saturday Review,* and *Time,* and it generated requests for hundreds of thousands of reprints.

As always, the Fund used events to heighten the effect of the advertising. In September 1969, Nelson Rockefeller was expected to make public a report on a survey trip he had made earlier in the year to Latin America on President Nixon's behalf. Contrary to expectations, the President refused to permit release of the report and the press began to buzz with speculations. The Fund quickly capitalized on the public attention being given Latin America by publishing an ad headlined "Latin American Aid Nullified by Population Explosion." This ran in *The Washington Post* and *Star* and *The Wall Street Journal,* and was also merchan-

"Population growth is a world problem which no country can ignore"

—President Richard M. Nixon

Whatever your cause, it's a lost cause unless we control population.

At last an American President has acknowledged that it is his Administration's "clear responsibility to provide essential leadership" to control the flood of humanity that threatens to engulf the earth. President Nixon's July 18th message to Congress on the hazards of unchecked population growth brings the U.S. one step closer to meeting the most far-reaching crisis of our time.

"Today the world population is three and a half billion persons," the President told Congress. "It took many thousands of years to produce the first billion people; the next billion took a century; the third billion came after 30 years; the fourth will be produced in just 15....Over the next 30 years...the world's population could double!...With birth rates remaining high and with death rates dropping sharply, many countries of Latin America, Asia and Africa now grow 10 times as fast as they did a century ago."

There will be a hundred million more people in *our own country* in another 30 years or so. Whatever your present cause, it is a lost cause unless we check the population explosion. Good causes such as schools, churches, colleges, hospitals, museums, libraries, community chests, heart funds, and conservation will inevitably be swamped by too many people.

President Nixon's Proposals

The President has proposed that Congress set up a commission on "population growth and the American future." He has directed government agencies to:

1. Undertake additional research on birth-control methods of all types.

2. Train more people to work in population and family-planning programs, both in this country and abroad.

3. Give the highest priority to new techniques that can help safeguard the environment.

4. Establish as a national goal the provision of adequate family-planning services in the United States within the next five years for all those who want them but cannot afford them.

The President pointed out that we will, therefore, "have to increase the amount we are spending on population and family planning." Our Government currently spends on population programs less than 3% of the amount it spends on space explorations. And far less than 1% of the amount it spends on the military.

We will also have to break down barriers of illiteracy and misinformation by utilizing fully the modern communication techniques of television and other mass media.

Write President Nixon in your own words telling him you applaud his plans and *ask him to implement them without delay.* Also contact anyone else in Washington you think might be helpful. Write your newspaper editor and talk to your friends, asking them to help. Your Government needs everyone's support in taking this courageous step in controlling population.

We'll be glad to send you reprints of this ad for posting where others will see it or for mailing to friends. We'll also send you reprints of President Nixon's message to Congress.

Remember: *Whatever your cause, it's a lost cause unless we control population.*

dized among people with personal interests in Latin American affairs and in the ad's strong population control message. It brought an enthusiastic reaction, including an offer from a Spanish-language magazine publisher to carry Hugh Moore Fund advertising free in his publication.

Through the years it had been a guiding conviction with Hugh Moore that, if he spoke vigorously about the danger ahead, his fellow Americans might understand and begin appropriate action. By experiment, he had found that dramatic yet soberly direct advertising in selected media did indeed bring action from the nation's leaders. Advertising was, in fact, Moore's most consistently used device to achieve the awakening he knew to be necessary.

Efforts for "Earth Day"

But Hugh Moore also sought other currents of effort that might contribute to the groundswell of public interest, which was finally becoming widely manifest as the new decade began. The nation-wide Environmental Teach-In, planned for April 22, 1970, seemed

FAIRFIELD OSBORN, the naturalist whose 1948 volume *Our Plundered Planet* gave warning of environmental disaster, was a longtime supporter of the Hugh Moore Fund.

THE ATTAINMENT of world peace has been Hugh Moore's chief motivation in his decades-long efforts for population control. But another strong stimulus has been his lifelong concern for the environment. Here he and Mrs. Moore stand at an entrance to the Hugh Moore Parkway, a 250-acre public park at the confluence of the Delaware and Lehigh Rivers that he assisted Easton, Pennsylvania, his home town, to acquire and develop.

to offer possibilities. But, as Moore read the early plans, the Teach-In appeared to lack any strong population component. Population control was mentioned, but seldom emphasized, and almost never given stature as the basic factor necessary to reverse the decline of the environment. He set out to help change this.

First, a third of a million leaflets, folders, and pamphlets (including a new pictorial edition of the venerable *Population Bomb*) were produced for campus and community distribution. Next, three efforts stressed the intimate relation between overpopulation and a degraded environment. One was the free distribution to 300-odd college radio stations of a taped radio program featuring Paul Ehrlich and David Brower. The second was provision, for reproduction free by college newspapers, of a score of editorial cartoons highlighting the population crisis. The third was a contest, conducted on over 200 campuses, that awarded prizes for slogans relating environmental troubles to "popullution."

Successful as these pre-Earth-Day efforts on campuses seemed to be, Hugh Moore felt that, unless not only the young but also those in power were made conscious of population's critical relation to the environment, an opportunity would be lost. He turned again to space advertising. Knowing that the signers of an ad could speak out more forcefully as private citizens than in the name of a foundation, Moore decided to pay for an advertisement out of his private resources. Over an appealing picture of a newborn infant, he addressed another open letter to President Nixon: "We can't lick the environment problem without considering this little fellow," it began. The signatures included many of the illustrious names that had signed earlier Campaign and Fund ads, but the coupon was directed to Hugh Moore personally.

The advertisement ran as a full page in *The New York Times* and *The Washington Post* just prior to Earth Day. It precipitated a magazine article, brought requests for thousands of reprints, and won immediate offers of free republication elsewhere. Moore followed it with his customary "merchandising" by mail to selected lists.

This advertisement appeared in full-page space in The New York Times and The Washington Post

Dear President Nixon:

We can't lick the environment problem without considering this little fellow.

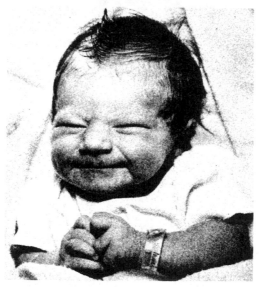

"**Every 7½ seconds** a new American is born. He is a disarming little thing, but he begins to scream loudly in a voice that can be heard for seventy years. He is screaming for 26,000,000 tons of water, 21,000 gallons of gasoline, 10,150 pounds of meat, 28,000 pounds of milk and cream, 9,000 pounds of wheat, and great storehouses of all other foods, drinks, and tobaccos. These are his life-time demands of his country and its economy." *Robert and Leona Train Rienow in Moment in the Sun*

We applaud your message to Congress, Mr. President, proposing a vast program to improve our environment. You said quite correctly that "While our population grows each one of us keeps using more of the earth's resources." You foresaw the need of spending more than *10 billion dollars* to purify our lakes and rivers, and additional billions to cleanse the air in this great country of ours.

But, Mr. President, this will be a losing battle unless we check our rapidly growing population, which is an underlying cause of the pollution of our environment.

Let's take a look at the growth of population in the United States:

1. We had 100 million people as recently as 1920 and never worried about the pollution of our environment.

2. However, we have added another 100 million people in the brief period since 1920.

3. And we shall add *still another 100 million* in the next thirty years or so at the present rate, bringing the total number up to 300 million people.

Today, with only 200 million, the water we drink may be contaminated and the air not fit to breathe. Noises deafen us. Our cities are packed with youngsters—thousands of them idle and victims of drug addiction. And millions more will pour into our streets in the years immediately ahead.

"Americans will be jammed together in an anthill society," according to your Secretary of Commerce, Mr. Maurice Stans, "unless government and business join in a coherent national growth policy."

Population Control Is Essential

Last year, Mr. President, you made a ringing pledge to provide leadership in the population field. You said, "When future generations evaluate...our time...one of the most important factors...will be the way we respond to population growth. Let us act in such a way that those who come after us...can do so with pride in the planet...with gratitude to those who lived on it in the past and with confidence in its future."

Notwithstanding your stirring words Congress has taken the best part of a year to authorize the Commission on Population Growth which you recommended. And we understand that the Family Assistance Program now under consideration would subsidize children at the rate of $300 for each child, *up to ten in many cases!*

We submit that a government which plans to spend *untold billions* to improve the environment for our present large population should not encourage large families. Indeed, there should be made available at least *$1 billion* to find and make known practical methods to enable humanity to control its numbers.

Proposed Measures To Control Population

These measures should include, among others, (1) improved methods of contraception, (2) basic research in the physiology of human reproduction, and (3) the utilization of modern communication techniques—radio, television and other mass media—to break down the barriers of illiteracy, ignorance and misinformation.

Population control must be a part of any forward-looking program to improve the environment. It should be among the very first steps to take, since the surging growth of population is basically responsible for the pollution of our environment.

ROBERT S. McNAMARA, World Bank
GEORGE CHAMPION,
   The Chase Manhattan Bank
THOMAS D. CABOT, Cabot Corporation
LAMMOT duP. COPELAND,
   E. I. duPont de Nemours & Co., Inc.
WILLIAM F. MAY, American Can Co.
FRANK W. ABRAMS,
   Standard Oil Co. of N.J.
HAROLD W. BOSTROM, UOP
   Transportation Equipment Group
JOHN COWLES, Minneapolis Star & Tribune

DR. L. H. FOSTER, Tuskegee Institute
WINTHROP W. ALDRICH,
   Ambassador to the Court of St. James's
HUGH MOORE, Dixie Cup Co.
GEN. WILLIAM H. DRAPER, JR.,
   Ambassador to NATO
DR. PHILIP M. HAUSER, University of Chicago
EMERSON FOOTE, Foote, Cone & Belding
MRS. ALBERT D. LASKER
RABBI WOLFE KELMAN,
   Rabbinical Assembly
MRS. CORDELIA S. MAY, Laurel Foundation

DR. REINHOLD NIEBUHR,
   Union Theological Seminary
DR. JOHN H. NORTHROP, Nobel Prize Winner
DAVID E. LILIENTHAL,
   Tennessee Valley Authority
JOHN ROCK, M.D., Harvard Medical School
ELMO ROPER, Public Opinion Analyst
THE RT. REV. HENRY KNOX
   SHERRILL, World Council of Churches
ERNEST L. STEBBINS, M.D.,
   Johns Hopkins University
LEWIS L. STRAUSS, Secretary of Commerce

The affiliations listed above do not necessarily imply the approval of the organizations mentioned. The individuals so designated are either currently, or were formerly, connected with those institutions.

Retrospect and Prospect

By 1970, Hugh Moore had personally spent well over 50 years in the quest for world peace, and the Hugh Moore Fund was entering a second quarter-century as his major instrument. When the Fund began, those who warned of overpopulation were little noticed or were scoffed at as "neo-Malthusians." (*Time* magazine, for instance, was a regular scoffer—technology, it held, would fix everything.) When William Vogt voiced his warnings in *The Road to Survival*, men of impeccable intellectual standing derided the book as "scare-mongering." Relatively few persons, intellectual or otherwise, bothered to examine or discuss population trends that professional demographers were already worrying about.

By 1970, however, Malthus' far-seeing wisdom was again being widely extolled. Most intellectuals now held overpopulation to be a precipitating factor in war, famine, resource exhaustion, pollution, and many of the other of the world's ills. Congress was now approving larger (though still far too small) budgets for family planning at home and abroad—$218.3 million budgeted for fiscal 1971 against an expenditure of only $29.2 million for 1967. And passage of the Tydings-Scheuer-Bush legislation in November, 1970, gave hope of far larger federal funding in future. The man in the street was beginning to be bombarded with TV discussions of population, with bumper-sticker messages ("Trouble Parking? Support Planned Parenthood"), with invitations to join organizations that plan political action (Zero Population Growth, Friends of the Earth), and with a plethora of magazine articles. The once-hostile *Time, Life,* and *Fortune* were by 1970 helping carry the educational burden, as were such other large-circulation publications as *Look, Reader's Digest, McCall's,* and *Redbook.* Indeed, it had become a measure of the movement's new stature in public awareness that leaders like General Draper and Hugh Moore were coming under personal attack by the far left (e.g., *Ramparts,* April 1970) and their warnings were being dismissed as "nonsense" by the far right (e.g., *National Review,* October 7,

1969) while the middle-of-the-road press was coming to embrace them as genuine prophets.

How much of the new awareness was the result of Hugh Moore's efforts? No man can say. But one *can* say that, throughout the nineteen fifties and sixties, no one else was proclaiming the coming danger as loudly, as often, or in as strategic places for the nation's leaders to hear as was Moore. In late 1969, the President of the United States made his estimate of Moore's contribution in a personal letter: "Your dedication to easing the problem of world population growth has led to a significant public service and the people of the world are in your debt."

Although, in 1970, Hugh Moore had to acknowledge that the prospects for arresting population growth still seemed dim, he continued to press forward the Fund's activities in the hope that we may yet avoid BREEDING OURSELVES TO DEATH.

APPENDIX A

COOPERATION OF LEADING AMERICANS

The following distinguished citizens from all walks of American life sponsored the campaign of the Hugh Moore Fund by signing one or more of the advertisements appearing in newspapers and magazines. (Signers acted in a personal capacity. Their affiliations, present or past, are given here for identification only.)

FRANK W. ABRAMS, Standard Oil Co. of N.J.

DR. JAMES LUTHER ADAMS, Harvard Divinity School

WINTHROP W. ALDRICH, U.S. Ambassador to Court of St. James's

GEORGE V. ALLEN, Foreign Service Institute, Department of State

DR. JOHN BARDEEN, Nobel Prize Winner

BRUCE BARTON, Batten, Barton, Durstine & Osborn

BISHOP STEPHEN F. BAYNE, JR., Vice President, Executive Council of the Episcopal Church

WALTER J. BERGMAN, Director, Owens Illinois

JAMES J. BIDDLE, Metropolitan Museum of Art

EUGENE R. BLACK, World Bank

REV. EUGENE CARSON BLAKE, United Presbyterian Church in the U.S.A.

JACOB BLAUSTEIN, U.S. Delegate to the United Nations

DR. GEORG BORGSTROM, Michigan State University

HAROLD W. BOSTROM, UOP Transportation Equipment Group

THOMAS C. BOUSHALL, The Bank of Virginia

DR. DETLEV W. BRONK, Rockefeller University

VAN WYCK BROOKS, Author

REV. ROBERT McAFEE BROWN, Stanford University

PERCIVAL F. BRUNDAGE, Director, Bureau of the Budget
ARTHUR H. BUNKER, American Metal Climax, Inc.
ELLSWORTH BUNKER, U.S. Ambassador to South Vietnam
DR. C. LALOR BURDICK, Christiana Foundation
THOMAS D. CABOT, Cabot Corporation
CASS CANFIELD, Harper & Row
REV. ALFORD CARLETON, The United Church Board for World
    Ministers
GEORGE CHAMPION, The Chase Manhattan Bank
STUART CHASE, Author
WILL L. CLAYTON, Under Secretary of State for Economic Affairs
RANDOLPH P. COMPTON, Kidder, Peabody & Co.
DR. EDWARD T. CONE, Princeton University
LAMMOT duP. COPELAND, E. I. duPont de Nemours & Co., Inc.
DR. LESLIE CORSA, JR., University of Michigan
JOHN COWLES, Minneapolis Star & Tribune
DR. JAMES A. CRABTREE, University of Pittsburgh
DR. WILLIAM V. D'ANTONIO, Notre Dame University
DONALD K. DAVID, The Ford Foundation
JAMES E. DAVIS, Winn-Dixie Stores, Inc.
DR. KINGSLEY DAVIS, U.S. Representative to the Population Com-
    mission of the United Nations
RAY P. DINSMORE, Goodyear Tire & Rubber Co.
GENERAL WILLIAM H. DRAPER, JR., Ambassador to NATO
ALEXANDER E. DUNCAN, Commercial Credit Co.
REYNOLDS duPONT, Senator, State of Delaware
DR. LOUIS DUPRE, Georgetown University
THEODORE EDISON
MARRINER S. ECCLES, Federal Reserve Board
RABBI MAURICE N. EISENDRATH, President, Union of Ameri-
    can Hebrew Congregations
MRS. ROBERT M. FERGUSON, International Planned Parenthood
    Federation
ROBERT B. FISKE, American Cyanamid Co.
HENRY C. FLOWER, JR., J. Walter Thompson Co.
MARION B. FOLSOM, Secretary of Health, Education and Welfare
EMERSON FOOTE, Foote, Cone & Belding
REV. HARRY EMERSON FOSDICK, Riverside Church
DR. L. H. FOSTER, President, Tuskegee Institute
ARTHUR B. FOYE, Haskins & Sells Foundation

RICHARD N. GARDNER, Deputy Assistant Secretary of State
L. HENRY GARLAND, M.D., University of California
CHAUNCEY B. GARVER, Shearman & Sterling
MRS. W. ST. JOHN GARWOOD
MRS. WALTER S. GIFFORD
ERNEST GRUENING, U.S. Senator from Alaska
JOHN GUNTHER, Author
ADMIRAL THOMAS C. HART, U.S.N.
DR. PHILIP M. HAUSER, University of Chicago
LELAND HAZARD, Carnegie Mellon University
WILLIAM RANDOLPH HEARST, JR., The Hearst Corporation
F. PEAVEY HEFFELFINGER, Peavey Co.
CHRISTIAN A. HERTER, Secretary of State
H. E. HUMPHREYS, JR., U.S. Rubber Co.
FANNIE HURST, Author
HENRY ITTLESON, JR., C.I.T. Financial Corp.
REV. R. CLAIBOURNE JOHNSON, American Baptist Convention
RABBI WOLFE KELMAN, The Rabbinical Assembly
DR. ANCEL P. KEYS, University of Minnesota
RABBI EDWARD E. KLEIN, Stephen Wise Free Synagogue
SHERMAN R. KNAPP, Connecticut Light & Power Co.
JOSEPH WOOD KRUTCH, Author
RICHARD S. KYLE, American Cyanamid Co.
THOMAS S. LAMONT, Morgan Guaranty Trust Co.
MRS. ALBERT D. LASKER
DR. CHAUNCEY D. LEAKE, American Association for the Advance-
ment of Science
MARX LEVA, Assistant Secretary of Defense
THE RT. REV. ARTHUR C. LICHTENBERGER, Episcopal
Church
DAVID E. LILIENTHAL, Tennessee Valley Authority
JOHN L. LOEB, Carl M. Loeb, Rhoades & Co.
BISHOP JOHN WESLEY LORD, The Methodist Church, Washing-
ton Area
MRS. CLARE BOOTHE LUCE
DAVID L. LUKE, West Virginia Pulp & Paper Co.
DR. ARCHIBALD MacLEISH, Harvard University
DR. ARNAUD C. MARTS, Bucknell University
MRS. CORDELIA S. MAY, Laurel Foundation
WILLIAM F. MAY, American Can Co.

FOWLER McCORMICK, International Harvester Co.
ROBERT S. McNAMARA, World Bank
DR. SAMUEL H. MILLER, Harvard Divinity School
DR. ASHLEY MONTAGU, Anthropologist
DR. WILLIAM E. MORAN, JR., Population Reference Bureau
DR. HERMANN J. MULLER, Nobel Prize Winner
CLIFFORD C. NELSON, The American Assembly
ALLAN NEVINS, Historian
DR. REINHOLD NIEBUHR, Union Theological Seminary
DR. JOHN H. NORTHROP, Nobel Prize Winner
FAIRFIELD OSBORN, Conservation Foundation
DR. LINUS PAULING, Nobel Prize Winner
MRS. PHILIP W. PILLSBURY
DR. GREGORY PINCUS, Worcester Foundation for Experimental
    Biology
FRANCIS T. P. PLIMPTON, Deputy U.S. Representative to the
    United Nations
ROCKEFELLER PRENTICE
ADMIRAL ARTHUR H. RADFORD, U.S.N.
EDWARD V. RICKENBACKER, Eastern Air Lines, Inc.
JOHN ROCK, M.D., Harvard Medical School
MRS. ELEANOR ROOSEVELT
ELMO ROPER
LESSING J. ROSENWALD
ALBERT B. SABIN, M.D., Cincinnati College of Medicine
JONAS SALK, M.D., The Salk Institute for Biological Studies
HARRY S. SCHERMAN, Book-of-the-Month Club
ADOLPH W. SCHMIDT, T. Mellon & Sons
M. LINCOLN SCHUSTER, Simon & Schuster
CHARLES E. SCRIPPS, Scripps-Howard Newspapers
DR. CLARENCE SENIOR, Brooklyn College
GEORGE CHEEVER SHATTUCK, M.D., Harvard School of Public
    Health
THE RT. REV. HENRY KNOX SHERRILL, World Council of
    Churches
DR. JOHN CRAYTON SNYDER, Harvard University
ERNEST L. STEBBINS, M.D., The Johns Hopkins University
LEWIS L. STRAUSS, Secretary of Commerce
SIDNEY A. SWENSRUD, Gulf Oil Corp.
CHARLES P. TAFT, Mayor of Cincinnati

DR. HAROLD C. UREY, Nobel Prize Winner
WILLIAM H. VANDERBILT, Governor of Rhode Island
MARK VAN DOREN, Author
CHARLES WHITE, Republic Steel Corp.
THE REV. CARL J. WESTMAN, Unitarian-Universalist Church
DR. PASCAL K. WHELPTON, Scripps Foundation
DR. JEROME B. WIESNER, Massachusetts Institute of Technology
MRS. FIFIELD WORKUM, Margaret Sanger Research Bureau
DR. HENRY M. WRISTON, Columbia University
DR. DON M. L. YOST, California Institute of Technology

APPENDIX B
SOME REPRESENTATIVE ADS

THE NEW YORK TIMES

THREAT TO PEACE

How can one helpless child possibly affect the peace of the world?

When you multiply him by 2 million—the number of children born every week in the world—the problem begins to come into focus.

Births now so far exceed deaths, due to world-wide health measures, that 70 million people are added to the earth's population annually.

This means that still another billion people will appear on this small planet of ours within the next 15 years—unless something is done about it.

More than half the people alive today are poorly fed and housed. With the flood of humanity now inundating the earth it is easy to see that we are headed for a period of famine, unrest, riots and probably war—which may make our experience in Vietnam seem minor by comparison.

It is only being realistic to say that skyrocketing population growth may doom the world we live in.

The accompanying chart reflects the relatively small amount of attention the population emergency is currently receiving from our Government. President Johnson is now proposing an increase of $25 million annually, but that is minuscule in terms of the total need.

This is your problem and you can do something about it. Tear out this ad and send it to anyone in Washington you think might be helpful. Urge the Government to initiate a crash program to deal with the population problem. And write us for two things: (1) Measures the Government can take to implement such a program. (2) Additional things you can do to help.

We can't afford to wait much longer. Every day lost only compounds the problem. The time to act is now.

CURRENT GOVERNMENT PROGRAMS
(1968 Estimates from 1969 Budget)

Space Program	$5 billion
Grants to States for Welfare	$3 billion
Health and Death Control Programs	$2.5 billion
Food for Peace Exports	$1.2 billion
Supersonic Plane (Pilot Model)	$170 million
Water and Air Pollution Control	$150 million
Crime Control	$100 million
Rat Control	$50 million
Population Control (United States)	$35 million
Population Control (foreign)	$35 million

CAMPAIGN TO CHECK THE POPULATION EXPLOSION
EMERSON FOOTE, CHAIRMAN

CAMPAIGN TO CHECK THE POPULATION EXPLOSION
60 EAST 42ND STREET
NEW YORK, N.Y. 10017   PHONE: (212) 986-6469
☐ Please send me more information and tell me how I can help.
☐ Please send me ____ free reprints of this ad.
NAME
ADDRESS
CITY _____ STATE _____ ZIP

EUGENE R. BLACK, former head, World Bank
HAROLD W. BOSTROM, UOP Transportation Equipment Group
DR. DETLEV BRONK, President, Rockefeller University
THOMAS D. CABOT, Cabot Corporation
GENERAL WILLIAM H. DRAPER, JR., former Ambassador to NATO
MARRINER S. ECCLES, former Chairman, Federal Reserve Board
ROBERT B. FISKE, Director, Pillsbury Company
HARRY EMERSON FOSDICK, Pastor Emeritus, Riverside Church

DR. PHILIP M. HAUSER, University of Chicago
LELAND HAZARD, Pittsburgh Plate Glass Co.
RABBI WOLFE KELMAN, The Rabbinical Assembly
JOSEPH WOOD KRUTCH, Author
MRS. ALBERT D. LASKER
MRS. CORDELIA S. MAY
DR. ASHLEY MONTAGU, Anthropologist
HUGH MOORE, former Chairman, St. Lawrence Seaway
DR. REINHOLD NIEBUHR, Union Theological Seminary
JOHN NUVEEN
DR. LINUS PAULING, Nobel Laureate

FRANCIS T. P. PLIMPTON, former Deputy U.S. Rep. to the United Nations
ROCKEFELLER PRENTICE
JOHN ROCK, M.D., Harvard Medical School
ELMO ROPER, Public Opinion Analyst
JONAS SALK, Director, The Salk Institute
ADOLPH W. SCHMIDT, T. Mellon & Sons
CHARLES E. SCRIPPS, Chairman, Scripps-Howard Newspapers
LEWIS L. STRAUSS, former Secretary of Commerce
ROBERT G. WEHLE, Genesee Brewing Company
DR. DON M. YOST, California Institute of Technology

THE POPULATION BOMB KEEPS TICKING

Those signing this statement do so in their personal and individual capacity. The institutional and business affiliations are purely descriptive carrying no implication of authorization or participation by the organization noted.

Good morning.
While you were asleep last night 3,336 people died from starvation.

You probably got about 8 hours sleep last night. From the time you got to bed to the time you got up this morning, 3,336 people in the underdeveloped nations died of illness caused by malnutrition. Mostly children.

You see, world population has <u>already</u> outgrown world food supply. And it's only the beginning. At the present rate, world population will increase by 70 million this year. 300 million in 4 years. One billion in 15 years. And <u>double</u> in 30 years. There will be <u>twice</u> as many mouths to feed. And no way in sight for us to feed them.

And mass starvation isn't the only threat. A hungry, over-crowded world will be a world of fear, chaos, poverty, riots, crime and war. No country will be safe. Not even our own. (It's beginning to hit home right now.)

What can we do about it? A <u>crash</u> program is needed to control population growth both at home and abroad. A White House Panel has recommended that the United States Government take the following steps <u>immediately</u> to meet the population emergency: A) Help develop and test new contraceptives and their accepti-

bility. B) Furnish contraceptives in quantity to underde-veloped countries requesting them. C) Investigate cultural attitudes and motivations toward family planning. D) Give greater support to the birth control programs of the United Nations and other groups working in this field.

Yet in fiscal 1967 we appropriated more for rat con-trol than birth control. 150 times more to help feed the underdeveloped nations than to help them solve the basic cause of their problems—their swelling populations.

We must go all out to control population growth

both at home and abroad. Not only for the sake of the starving of the world. But for our own sake. And the sake of our children. It's the best, most humanitarian, least expensive way we know to secure the future peace and prosperity of our nation. And our world.

What can <u>you</u> do to help? Many things. Write us and we'll tell you about them. And send this ad to anyone in Washington you think might be helpful. Urge the Gov-ernment to speed up action in the population crisis.

It's time to wake up. We've been asleep too long.

CAMPAIGN TO CHECK THE POPULATION EXPLOSION
EMERSON FOOTE, CHAIRMAN

CAMPAIGN TO CHECK THE POPULATION EXPLOSION
60 EAST 42ND STREET
NEW YORK, N.Y. 10017   PHONE: (212) 986-6469
☐ I'm interested. Tell me how I can help.
☐ Please send me more information.
☐ Please send me____ free reprints of this ad. 14

NAME_____

ADDRESS_____

CITY_____STATE_____ZIP_____

DR. DETLEV BRONK, President, Rockefeller University
MRS. ALBERT D. LASKER
DR. HAROLD C. UREY, Nobel Prize Winner
FRANK W. ABRAMS, former Chairman, Standard Oil Co. of N.J.
WINTHROP W. ALDRICH, former U.S. Ambassador to Court of St-James
THURMAN W. ARNOLD, former Assistant U.S. Attorney General
HAROLD W. BOSTROM, Vice President,
    UOP Transportation Equipment Group
JACOB BLAUSTEIN, former Delegate to the United Nations
THOMAS D. CABOT, Chairman, Cabot Corporation
JOHN COWLES, President, Minneapolis Star & Tribune
GENERAL WILLIAM H. DRAPER, JR., former Ambassador to NATO

MARRINER S. ECCLES, former Chairman, Federal Reserve Board
HENRY C. FLOWER, JR., former Vice Chairman, J. Walter Thompson Co.
HENRY ITTLESON, JR., Chairman, C.I.T. Financial Corp.
JOSEPH WOOD KRUTCH, Author
FOWLER McCORMICK, former Chairman,
    International Harvester Co.
HUGH MOORE, former Chairman, St. Lawrence Seaway Corporation
ALLAN NEVINS, President, American Academy of Arts & Letters
DR. REINHOLD NIEBUHR, Professor Emeritus,
    Union Theological Seminary
FRANCIS T. P. PLIMPTON, former Ambassador
    and Deputy U.S. Rep. to the United Nations

ROCKEFELLER PRENTICE
ELMO ROPER, Public Opinion Analyst
LESSING J. ROSENWALD
JONAS SALK, M.D., Director, The Salk Institute for Biological Studies
ADOLPH W. SCHMIDT, Governor, T. Mellon & Sons
DR. WILLIAM SHOCKLEY, Nobel Laureate
CHARLES P. TAFT, former Mayor of Cincinnati
WILLIAM H. VANDERBILT, former Governor
    of Rhode Island
MARK VAN DOREN, Author
ROBERT G. WEHLE, Treasurer,
    Genesee Brewing Company

THE
POPULATION BOMB
KEEPS TICKING

These signing this statement do so in their personal and individual capacity. The institutional and business affiliations are purely descriptive carrying no implication of authorization or participation by the organization noted.

THE NEW YORK TIMES

A Recent Gallup Poll Shows:

THE AMERICAN PEOPLE OVERWHELMINGLY FAVOR BIRTH CONTROL.

Americans were asked whether or not they felt birth control information should be available to anyone who wants it. Here's what they said:

GALLUP SURVEY			
CATHOLICS		NON-CATHOLICS	
YES	73%	YES	77%
NO	22%	NO	18%
NO OPINION	5%	NO OPINION	5%

The quality of living in America—as well as the peace of the world—is threatened by the Population Explosion.

As our numbers grow, the water we drink becomes more polluted day by day. The very air we breathe may endanger our health. And we go out at night in our over-crowded cities at the risk of life and limb.

A few years ago who would have dreamed that such things could happen in this great country of ours. But they have.

And in the world around us the situation is even more serious. Each week over a million babies are born. In ten years there will be one billion more—1,000 million! (That's five times the present population of the United States.) And most of them will not have enough to eat. Birth Control is the only answer. Yet the chart at the right reflects what little attention it is receiving from our Government. A fraction of the vast amounts we spend on health and welfare would not only help reduce those costs but help check the population explosion. (And, incidentally, help balance the badly unbalanced national budget. And save money for overburdened taxpayers.)

The Gallup Poll shows that the American people would overwhelmingly support such a program.

This is your problem and you can do something about it. Tear out this ad and send it to anyone in Washington you think might be helpful. Urge the Government to initiate a <u>crash program</u> for population stabilization. And write us for two things. (1) Measures the Government can take to implement such a program. (2) Additional things <u>you</u> can do to help.

We can't afford to wait much longer. Every day lost only compounds the problem. The time to act is <u>now</u>.

CURRENT GOVERNMENT PROGRAMS
(1968 Estimates from 1969 Budget)

Space Program	$5 billion
Grants to States for Welfare	$5 billion
Health and Death Control Programs	$2.6 billion
Food for Peace Exports	$1.2 billion
Supersonic Plane (Pilot Model)	$170 million
Air Pollution	$100 million
Crime Control	$100 million
Rat Control	$50 million
Population Control (United States)	$35 million
Population Control (Foreign)	$35 million

CAMPAIGN TO CHECK THE POPULATION EXPLOSION
EMERSON FOOTE, CHAIRMAN

CAMPAIGN TO CHECK THE POPULATION EXPLOSION
60 EAST 42ND STREET
NEW YORK, N.Y. 10017   PHONE: (212) 986-6469
☐ Please send me more information and tell me how I can help.
☐ Please send me free reprints of this ad.   1A
NAME_____
ADDRESS_____
CITY_____STATE_____ZIP

EUGENE R. BLACK, former head, World Bank
MRS. ALBERT D. LASKER
GEORGE V. ALLEN, former Director, U. S. Information Agency
FRANK W. ABRAMS, former Chairman, Standard Oil Co. of N.J.
DR. JACQUES BARZUN, Professor, Columbia University
THOMAS D. CABOT, Cabot Foundation, Inc.
JOHN COWLES, President, Minneapolis Star and Tribune
DR. LOUIS DUPRÉ, Georgetown University
MARRINER S. ECCLES, former Chairman, Federal Reserve Board
ROBERT B. FISKE, Director, Pillsbury Company
HARRY EMERSON FOSDICK, Pastor Emeritus, Riverside Church

DR. PHILIP M. HAUSER, University of Chicago
RABBI WOLFE KELMAN, Executive Vice President, The Rabbinical Assembly
MRS. CORDELIA MAY
FOWLER McCORMICK, former Chairman, International Harvester Co.
DR. ASHLEY MONTAGU, Anthropologist
DR. JOHN H. NORTHROP, Nobel Laureate
JOHN ROCK, M.D. Harvard Medical School
LESSING J. ROSENWALD
ALBERT S. SABIN, M.D., Cincinnati College of Medicine
A. W. SCHMIDT, Governor, T. Mellon & Sons
DR. WILLIAM SHOCKLEY, Nobel Laureate

LEWIS L. STRAUSS, former Secretary of Commerce
HAROLD W. BOSTROM, UOP Transportation Equipment Group
GENERAL WILLIAM H. DRAPER, JR., former Ambassador to NATO
HENRY C. FLOWER, JR. former Vice Chairman, J. Walter Thompson Co.
HUGH MOORE, former Chairman, St. Lawrence Seaway Corporation
ROCKEFELLER PRENTICE
ELMO ROPER, Public Opinion Analyst
ROBERT G. WEHLE, Treasurer, Genesee Brewing Company

THE POPULATION BOMB KEEPS TICKING

These signing this statement do so in their personal and individual capacity. The institutional and business affiliations are purely descriptive carrying no implication of authorization or participation by the organization named.

THE POPULATION BOMB THREATENS THE PEACE OF THE WORLD

SO WHAT ARE WE DOING ABOUT IT?

Fifteen years ago there were 2.5 billion people on earth. Today there are 3.5 billion—and newcomers are arriving on the scene at the net rate of more than <u>one million a week</u>! In another fifteen short years there will be at least 4.5 billion people on this small planet of ours. Most of them hungry. And make no mistake about it, America cannot long remain an island of prosperity in a sea of poverty and hunger.

If corrective measures to check this human flood are not taken right here and now the resulting world-wide misery, strife, revolutions and

wars will make our experience in Viet Nam appear minor by comparison.

The population crisis is the greatest problem humanity faces. And the National Academy of Sciences has said that the Population Bomb "can be successfully attacked by developing new methods of fertility regulation and implementing programs of family planning widely and rapidly throughout the world." Yet the accompanying chart reflects the scant amount of attention the population problem is currently receiving from our Government.

This is your problem and you can do something about it. Tear out this ad and send it to anyone in Washington you think might be helpful. Urge the Government to initiate a <u>crash program</u> for population stabilization. And write us for two things: (1) Measures the Government can take to implement such a program. (2) Additional things <u>you</u> can do to help.

We can't afford to wait very much longer. Every day lost will only compound the population problem.

The time to act is <u>now</u>.

CURRENT GOVERNMENT PROGRAMS	
(1969 Estimates from 1970 Budget)	
Space Program	$4 billion
Grants to States for Welfare	$3.4 billion
Federal Health Programs	$11 billion
Food for Peace Exports	$900 million
Supersonic Aircraft	$126 million
Air Pollution	$85 million
Crime Control	$639 million
Population Control (United States)	$65 million
Population Control (Foreign)	$51 million

CAMPAIGN TO CHECK THE POPULATION EXPLOSION
60 EAST 42nd STREET, NEW YORK, NEW YORK 10017
EMERSON FOOTE, CHAIRMAN

THE NEW YORK TIMES, SUNDAY NOVEMBER 24, 1968   5 E

Dear President-Elect Nixon:
The underlying problem facing your administration will not be war, riots or crime, but the population bomb

In the four year term of office to which you have been elected there will be *ten million more* Americans—most of them living in our already over-crowded cities.

And there will be *three hundred million more* people in the world at the present rate of increase—most of them without enough to eat.

Fourteen million people will die of starvation during your term of office unless the present death rate of ten thousand a day is reduced. (America cannot feed the world, as we have found after shipping $15 billion worth of food abroad in recent years.)

There were 2½ billion people in the world in 1953. Today only 15 years later there are *one billion more!* This basic problem, Mr. President, bears directly or indirectly on most of the problems you will have to deal with during your Administration.

To check the population explosion —both in this country and abroad— you must seek appropriations many times larger than those heretofore allocated for birth control by our Govern-ment. Surely a nation which approves $1½ billion to develop a new military airplane can afford to devote a comparable sum to the solution of the most urgent problem of the human race!

For there is little doubt that unless population is brought under control *at an early date* the resulting social tensions and misery will inevitably lead to chaos and strife—to revolutions and wars which may make our present expe-rience in Vietnam minor by comparison.

Nothing less than the survival of civilization is in the balance.

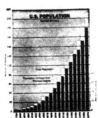

CAMPAIGN TO CHECK THE POPULATION EXPLOSION
EMERSON FOOTE, CHAIRMAN

FRANK W. ABRAMS, former Chairman,
  Standard Oil Co. of New Jersey
EUGENE R. BLACK, former head, World Bank
HAROLD W. BOSTROM, UOP Transportation
  Equipment Group
JOHN COWLES, Chairman, Minneapolis Star & Tribune
MRS. ALBERT D. LASKER
GEORGE V. ALLEN, former Director,
  U.S. Information Agency
DR. JACQUES BARZUN, Columbia University

VIRGINIUS DABNEY,
  Editor, Richmond Times-Dispatch
GENERAL WILLIAM H. DRAPER, JR.,
  former Ambassador to NATO
DR. LOUIS DUPRE, Georgetown University
MARRINER S. ECCLES, former head,
  Federal Reserve System
HENRY C. FLOWER, JR., former Vice Chairman,
  J. Walter Thompson Co.
DR. PHILIP M. HAUSER, University of Chicago

LELAND HAZARD, Pittsburgh Plate Glass Co.
RABBI WOLFE KELMAN, The Rabbinical Assembly
MRS. CORDELIA S. MAY, Laurel Foundation
DR. ASHLEY MONTAGU, Anthropologist
HUGH MOORE, former Chairman, St. Lawrence Seaway
DR. LINUS PAULING, Nobel Laureate
FRANCIS T. P. PLIMPTON, former Ambassador
  and Deputy U.S. Rep. to the United Nations
ROCKEFELLER PRENTICE
JOHN ROCK, M.D., Harvard Medical School

ELMO ROPER, Public Opinion Analyst
ALBERT E. SABIN, M.D.,
  Cincinnati College of Medicine
ADOLPH W. SCHMIDT, T. Mellon & Sons
CHARLES E. SCRIPPS, Chairman,
  Scripps-Howard Newspapers
LEWIS L. STRAUSS, former Secretary of Commerce
CHARLES P. TAFT, former Mayor of Cincinnati
ROBERT G. WEHLE, Genesee Brewing Company
DR. DON YOST, California Institute of Technology

THE NEW YORK TIMES

HAVE YOU EVER BEEN MUGGED? WELL, YOU MAY BE!

There is an aggravated assault in this country every 3 minutes. A forcible rape every 26 minutes. A murder every hour—11,000 a year.

These are the ones that have been reported. The Presidential Crime Commission estimates that several times that number are unreported.

This has come with the population explosion in the United States, where our numbers have doubled—from 100 million people to more than 200 million people—in the lifetime of many of us.

City slums—jam-packed with juveniles, thousands of them idle—breed discontent, drug addiction and chaos. And crime in the cities is not the only problem. We have air and water pollution in wide areas. And the quality of life in this great country of ours is deteriorating before our eyes with the rapid increase of people.

Is there an answer? Yes—birth control is one.

And the quicker the better. For the population explosion if not checked will compound itself—adding millions of idle youngsters to our streets—in just a few short years.

A fraction of the vast amounts we spend on health and welfare if devoted to birth control could help check our skyrocketing numbers. And incidentally, help balance the badly imbalanced national budget and save money for hard-pressed taxpayers.

President Johnson has said that the population problem is the greatest humanity faces. Yet the accompanying chart reflects the amount of attention it is actually getting. The expenditures this year are more than last, but they are pitifully small considering the dimensions of the problem—and may quite likely be too late.

What can you do about it? Tear out this ad and send it to anyone in Washington you think might be helpful. Urge the Government to initiate a crash program for population stabilization. And write us for a list of things the Government can do to implement such a program. And a list of things you can do to help.

Do it now. Before you walk home tonight.

CURRENT GOVERNMENT PROGRAMS (1968 Estimates from 1969 Budget)	
Space Program	$5.5 billion
Grants to States for Welfare	$3 billion
Health and Death Control Programs	$2.5 billion
Food for Peace Exports	$1.2 billion
Supersonic Plane (Pilot Model)	$170 million
Air Pollution	$100 million
Crime Control	$100 million
Riot Control	$50 million
Population Control (United States)	$35 million
Population Control (Foreign)	$35 million

CAMPAIGN TO CHECK THE POPULATION EXPLOSION
60 EAST 42ND STREET
NEW YORK, N.Y. 10017   PHONE: (212) 986-6469
☐ Please send me more information and tell me how I can help.
☐ Please send me   free reprints of this ad.   14
NAME
ADDRESS
CITY_____ STATE_____ ZIP

CAMPAIGN TO CHECK THE POPULATION EXPLOSION
EMERSON FOOTE, CHAIRMAN

EUGENE R. BLACK, former head, World Bank
MRS. ALBERT D. LASKER
HAROLD W. BOSTROM, Vice President,
   UOP Transportation Equipment Group
THOMAS D. CABOT, Chairman, Cabot Corporation
JOHN COWLES, President, Minneapolis Star Tribune
FRANK W. ABRAMS, former Chairman,
   Standard Oil Co. of N.J.

GENERAL WILLIAM H. DRAPER, JR.,
   former Ambassador to NATO
MARRINER S. ECCLES, former Chairman,
   Federal Reserve Board
HENRY C. FLOWER, JR., former Vice Chairman,
   J. Walter Thompson Co.,
HARRY EMERSON FOSDICK, Pastor Emeritus,
   Riverside Church

JOSEPH WOOD KRUTCH, Author
HUGH MOORE, former Chairman,
   St. Lawrence Seaway Corporation
ROCKEFELLER PRENTICE
ELMO ROPER, Public Opinion Analyst
LESSING J. ROSENWALD
ADOLPH W. SCHMIDT, Governor, T. Mellon & Sons
ROBERT O. WEHLE, Treasurer, Genesee Brewing Company

THE POPULATION BOMB KEEPS TICKING

Those signing this statement do so in their personal and individual capacity. The institutional and business affiliations are purely descriptive carrying no implication of authorization or participation by the organization named.

THE NEW YORK TIMES

How many people do you want in your country?

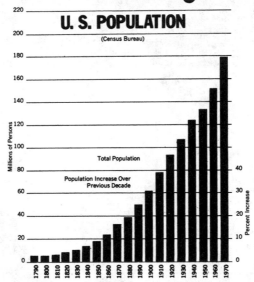

U. S. POPULATION
(Census Bureau)

Millions of Persons

Total Population

Population Increase Over Previous Decade

Percent Increase

The above chart shows the increase in the United States population by decades, prepared by the Census Bureau.
Examine it closely. You will see:

That our population was 100 million as recently as 1920.

That we have added another 100 million since that date.

We shall add approximately another 100 million in the next 35 years at the present rate of increase. This will bring the total number of Americans to 300 million!

Conditions in the United States Today

Let's take a look at conditions in our country as they exist today with our present population of 200 million Americans.

Our waters—rivers, lakes and beaches—are polluted. We are literally deafened by noise, and poisoned by carbon monoxide from 100 million cars.

Our city slums are packed with youngsters—thousands of them idle, victims of discontent and drug addiction. And millions more will pour into our streets in the next few years at the present rate of procreation.

You go out after dark at your peril. Last year one out of every four hundred Americans was murdered, raped or robbed.

Birth Control is an Answer

Our authorities in Washington have given relatively little attention to the population problem—as you can see from the adjoining table. However, a high-level Presidential Committee after months of study has now come up

with recommendations of practical measures which can be taken to help stabilize our numbers. These include improved methods of contraception, basic research on the physiology of reproduction, and the utilization of modern communications techniques—television and other mass media—for breaking down the barriers of illiteracy and misinformation.

Write us for a summary of these recommendations. And send this advertisement to President Nixon urging him to institute a crash program to deal with the population problem without delay. Also contact anyone else in Washington you think might be helpful.

It is up to you—and citizens like you—to decide how many people you want in the United States. The well-being of your children and your children's children depends on you.

CURRENT FEDERAL PROGRAMS IN MILLIONS OF DOLLARS (APPROXIMATE)	
DEFENSE	$90,000
FEDERAL HEALTH PROGRAMS	$10,000
SPACE PROGRAM	$ 4,000
WELFARE GRANTS TO STATES	$ 3,000
POPULATION PROGRAMS*	$ 116

Man's greatest problem is the fearful race between food and population. If we lose that race our hopes for the future will turn to ashes. —FORMER PRESIDENT JOHNSON

CAMPAIGN TO CHECK THE POPULATION EXPLOSION
60 EAST 42nd STREET, NEW YORK, NEW YORK 10017
EMERSON FOOTE, CHAIRMAN

THE NEW YORK TIMES

WARNING:
THE WATER YOU ARE DRINKING MAY BE POLLUTED

Much of our drinking water is below Federal standards according to a recent study.

Two things are causing this rise in water pollution. One is the increase in waste products. Every day we pour thousands of tons of sewage, garbage, toxic chemicals, insecticides, herbicides and industrial discharges into our water. It is literally enough to make you sick!

But the basic cause is the rising population of the United States. As recently as 1920 we had only 100 million people. Since that date we have added another 100 million! And at the present rate of increase there will be a third 100 million in 30 or 35 years.

The rising tide of people in impoverished countries is even greater—constituting a threat to the peace of the world in which we live.

Hundreds of millions of people actually do not have enough to eat. There is the prospect of social upheavals, revolutions and wars in Latin America, Asia and elsewhere unless this rising flood of humanity can be controlled.

This urgent problem is receiving relatively little attention from our Government, as you can see from the accompanying table. However, a high-level Presidential Committee after months of study has now come up with recommendations of practical measures which can be taken to help stabilize our numbers. These include improved methods of contraception,

basic research on the physiology of reproduction, and the utilization of modern communications techniques—television and other mass media—for breaking down the barriers of illiteracy and misinformation.

You may use the coupon on this page to obtain a summary of those recommendations. And send this advertisement to President Nixon urging him to institute a crash program to deal with the population problem without delay. Also contact anyone else in Washington you think might be helpful.

It is up to you—and citizens like you—to take action. The well-being of your children and your children's children is at stake.

CURRENT FEDERAL PROGRAMS IN MILLIONS OF DOLLARS (APPROXIMATE)	
DEFENSE	$80,000
FEDERAL HEALTH PROGRAMS	$10,000
SPACE PROGRAM	$ 4,000
WELFARE GRANTS TO STATES	$ 3,000
POPULATION PROGRAMS*	$ 116

*Man's greatest problem is the fearful race between food and population. If we lose that race our hopes for the future will turn to ashes. —FORMER PRESIDENT JOHNSON

CAMPAIGN TO CHECK THE POPULATION EXPLOSION
60 EAST 42nd STREET, NEW YORK, NEW YORK 10017
EMERSON FOOTE, CHAIRMAN

THE POPULATION BOMB KEEPS TICKING

APPENDIX C
SOME COLLECTIVE COMMENT

Excerpt from the minutes of the Executive Committee of the Western Hemisphere Region of the International Planned Parenthood Federation on the occasion of Hugh Moore's retirement, September 11, 1969:

> Mr. Hugh Moore, a pioneer in the population movement, retires from the Executive Committee as of this meeting.
>
> He established the Hugh Moore Fund in 1944 to promote world peace, but was one of the first to comprehend the relationship between population pressure and peace.
>
> Since 1954 his energies and his Fund's resources have been devoted to population control.
>
> Hugh Moore raised the first substantial funds for the International Planned Parenthood Federation by organizing the World Population Emergency Campaign in 1959. He provided the first paid staff for the Western Hemisphere Region and donated office space during its early struggles. In the opinion of this writer (Charles F. Brush), the W.H.R. might never have survived to become the potent and viable organization of today were it not for Hugh Moore. He has been a member of the W.H.R. Regional Council and Executive Committee from its inception in 1955, served on the I.P.P.F. Governing Body from 1957 to 1967, and was Vice President of the Governing Body from 1962 to 1967.
>
> Hugh Moore also founded the Population Crisis Committee, the Campaign to Check the Population Explo-

sion, and provided essential guidance and financial aid during the establishment of the Population Reference Bureau and the Association for Voluntary Sterilization, where he is Chairman of the Executive Committee.

Moved, seconded, and passed: That this Executive Committee proffers its thanks and deep appreciation to Hugh Moore for his many contributions to the I.P.P.F., the W.H.R., and the cause of family planning.

●

A resolution adopted on Hugh Moore's retirement from the Executive Committee of the Association for Voluntary Sterilization, December 2, 1969:

The Executive Committee of the Association for Voluntary Sterilization, individually and collectively, wishes to give you our deepest thanks and appreciation for your superb leadership of our organization.

First in your capacity as President of the Association, and then in your position as Chairman of the Executive Committee, you have served AVS with distinction. You have been the inspiration and driving force behind AVS for so long that whatever progress we have made stems in large part from your initiative and leadership. Your energy and ceaseless devotion are a constant marvel to all of us.

From a small organization, AVS has reached a point of sizable national influence, and every step bears the mark of your genius. The name of Hugh Moore will be inseparably linked with AVS and the whole movement for population control.

If we find it hard to think of this Committee without you at its helm, we hope this loss will be a matter of a title only, and that you will stay with us in this crusade that must succeed if you are part of it. We will honor you always not just for your leadership but your boundless wisdom and friendship.

APPENDIX D

HUGH MOORE'S
BUSINESS BACKGROUND

The Dixie Cup Company, an enterprise with eight plants valued at some $75 million when it merged with American Can Company in 1957, sprang from the brains of two boys from Kansas who arrived in New York in 1910 with an idea to sell. Fresh from Harvard, where they had planned their new business venture, Hugh Moore and Lawrence Luellen took a room at the prestigious Waldorf-Astoria and wrote letters to possible backers on the hotel's gold-embossed stationery. Then they opened an office in Wall Street and started a bank account with their slim savings at the Title Guarantee & Trust Company.

Arthur Terry, the bank's treasurer, on the theory that "Wall Street is full of skin games," asked with skepticism what they were selling. When they described the paper cup, he was impressed enough to send them to Edgar L. Marston, a partner in Blair & Co., an important investment firm, who occasionally went into visionary schemes. "I still remember the day," Moore has recalled, "when I walked into the marble reception room of Blair & Co.— all of 22 years of age—clutching my letter of introduction in one hand and a little pack of Dixie cups in the other." Marston later reported that Moore opened the interview by announcing: "Mr. Marston, do you know that it is very dangerous to drink out of the common drinking cup?"

It was the kind of shock technique he employed effectively all his life. The result was that Marston introduced him to W. T. Graham, president of the American Can Company; and Graham,

Marston and Percy Rockefeller put up $200,000 to launch the paper cup in the United States.

As always, this shock technique was backed by research. When he warned Marston of the danger of the common drinking glass and tin dipper, seldom washed and never sterilized, he knew that recent studies would prove the paper cup a boon to public health. Professor Alvin P. Davison, a biologist at Lafayette College, had already made experiments in Pennsylvania schools and found that disease could be communicated from one person to another on the rim of dirty glasses.

Dr. S. J. Crumbine, Health Officer of Kansas, had found that thousands of tubercular patients, who rode the trains through Kansas en route to the mountains of Colorado in the belief that altitude would cure them, were using the same drinking glasses as healthy passengers. Crumbine's laboratory experiments at the University of Kansas had convinced him that public drinking glasses were a health menace, and he ordered them abolished throughout the state.

Moore's campaign to sell paper cups met with stiff resistance. The general manager of a midwestern railroad, after listening to his story, snapped: "I have drunk out of unwashed glasses in railway cars, saloons and everywhere else, as my father did before me. I am 60 years old and in good health. Now pick up your little cups, son, and run along."

Health Officer Crumbine provided the needed opening. Although the politically powerful railroads, whose lines passed through Kansas, attacked him bitterly, the doctor stood firm, even sending his reports to health officers of other states. When Moore called on the Pullman Company in Chicago, the vice president complained that "this damn little health officer in Kansas has ordered us to take out the glasses we have always used, and we have nothing to take their place."

Moore had just what he needed—Dixie cups!

Soon other states followed Kansas in passing laws against the common drinking glass. Moore supported this health crusade—

and built Dixie's sales—with a little magazine he called "The Cup Campaigner." A frustrated journalist who had originally hoped to start a newspaper, he edited the magazine himself. With pungent pictures of disease-ridden men drinking from public glasses, and frequent quotations from health studies and laws that could eliminate this menace, he soon developed the dramatic style that would later characterize his pamphlets and advertisements for the population movement.

Dixie Cup's co-founder, Lawrence Luellen, left the business in its early years, distracted by other interests. Moore, with characteristic singleness of purpose, kept building the infant enterprise. In 1920 he moved its headquarters to Easton, Pennsylvania, and himself became an Easton resident. After World War I service as an Army captain, he returned to lead Dixie through prosperous years in the twenties and thirties despite the great depression.

By 1937 Moore was sharing his business burdens with a management team he had developed and was devoting his own time increasingly to public causes. The Dixie Cup Company, with 5,000 shareholders, was listed on the New York Stock Exchange.

In 1957 the American Can Company made an attractive offer of merger, which Dixie accepted. Moore continued, however, as a consultant to the company with an office in the Hugh Moore Plant, the headquarters of the Dixie Division of the American Can Company at Easton.

HUGH MOORE in a portrait by Frank Bensing. The picture hangs in the Hugh Moore Plant of the Dixie Cup Co. in Easton, Pennsylvania.

OBJECTIVE: WORLD PEACE

Hugh Moore served with the United States armed forces in the first World War. It was his wish that the foundation that bears his name might assist in the movement for world peace and that his descendents would be spared the horrors of war. But this wish has yet to be fulfilled as will be seen from the following.

CRAIG MOORE, son of the founder, served as an Air Force officer in the Second World War. He is Vice President and a Director of the Hugh Moore Fund.

HUGH MOORE, JR., son of the founder, was an officer in the Army in the Second World War as well as in the Korean War.

SCOTT MOORE, grandson of the founder, was awarded the Purple Heart, the Bronze Star, and the Army Medal for Bravery for his service in Viet Nam.

Purpose
of
Hugh Moore Fund

‡ ✦ ‡

To mobilize public interest in the population explosion with a view to stimulating research and education proportionate to its magnitude and importance — in the hope thereby of improving in some degree the quality of human life and of reducing social tensions and promoting Peace.

It should be expressly noted from the foregoing that our capital and income should be used to stimulate others — individuals, universities, foundations, governments, etc., to undertake research and education in depth.

It is obvious that the Fund itself is not equipped, either in resources or facilities, to pursue the vast job of research in human fertility and motivation that needs to be done.

November 8, 1961

HUGH MOORE FUND

INDEX